Note for Librarians: A cataloguing record for this book is available from Library and Archives Canada at www.collectionscanada.ca/amicus/index-e.html
ISBN 1-4251-0429-0

Offices in Canada, USA, Ireland and UK

Book sales for North America and international:
Trafford Publishing, 6E–2333 Government St.,
Victoria, BC V8T 4P4 CANADA
phone 250 383 6864 (toll-free 1 888 232 4444)
fax 250 383 6804; email to orders@trafford.com
Book sales in Europe:
Trafford Publishing (UK) Limited, 9 Park End Street, 2nd Floor
Oxford, UK OX1 1HH UNITED KINGDOM
phone +44 (0)1865 722 113 (local rate 0845 230 9601)
facsimile +44 (0)1865 722 868; info.uk@trafford.com
Order online at:
trafford.com/06-2186

10 9 8 7 6 5 4 3 2 1

Singh to Suresh: Non-Citizens, the Canadian Courts and Human Rights Obligations

by Tom Clark

2006

To the child who was able to say the emperor has no clothes ...

Acknowledgement

Human rights depend on many people in many situations. I was privileged to meet so many human rights advocates: people in the Justice Department; the human rights sections of Foreign Affairs and Heritage Canada; staff and members of human rights treaty bodies. So many of them were deeply committed to giving effect to human rights. They inspired and encouraged me.

This is not a scholarly book. That is, the book does not emerge from the context of the normative thinking of a community of scholars in a recognized academic discipline such as law. It is a book with the perspective of the bystander and activist looking independently at the court and at human rights body decisions. Such personal reflection need not rely on the latest book or article by those considered experts. Of course, it would be foolish to ignore the views of experts, but the book stands or falls by its own reflection on court or treaty body decisions.

Although not scholarly, the book would not have been possible without some training acquired over the years. My 1992 *Diplôme* from the International Institute of Human Rights in Strasbourg helped get me started on international comparative human rights. This has been augmented in Canada by interactions with a number of creative lawyers who shared a passion about the rights promised by the *Canadian Charter of Rights and Freedoms* and by international human rights.

I give a special thanks to Barbara Jackman who, from early discussions about the intervention to be made by the Canadian Council of Churches in *Singh et al* in 1984, took my layman's thoughts seriously. She gave effect to rights for individuals through the cases argued before Canadian

Courts and international human rights treaty bodies.

I owe another big thank you to the church representatives on the then Inter-Church Committee for Refugees and to the Board members of the Canadian Council of Churches who were willing to back our project of financing lawyers to promote fundamental rights of refugees and non-citizens before the courts and international treaty bodies. Among the many, I think especially of Nancy Nicholls, George Cram, Helga (then) Kutz-Harder, Ted Hyland and the late Charles Hay and Kathleen Ptolemy.

There are so many lawyers who, over the years, tried to set me straight on Canadian law. David Beatty gave educational testimony before the Senate hearings on Bills C55 & C84 around 1988. Craig Scott started me on my first human rights paper. Sharryn Aiken worked with me on articles and was a lawyer for other interveners in some of the cases. François Crépeau sorted out my thinking in two collaborations. Intervener lawyers in *Suresh* like Marlys Edwardh tried to correct my thinking on the *Charter*. Stephen Toope read an early draft and gave some guidance. However, none of these persons is responsible for my failings. Errors or residual misunderstandings and a stubborn streak are entirely mine.

Finally, I have to thank my family for helping with the book. My wife, Pat, did some copy editing. Cathy served as a sounding board. Andrew and Angie helped to get me started in the practicalities of publishing this way.

Thank you one and all!

Table of Contents

Chapter 1. Introduction

Beginning with Singh

This book follows a story which began one evening in 1984 in a Toronto living room. Lawyers wanted to meet with members of the then Inter-Church Committee for Refugees (ICCR) - a national ecumenical committee linked to the Canadian Council of Churches (CCC). Canadian lawyers had become involved with refugee affairs in Canada around the Chilean refugees following the collapse of democracy in Chile and the beginning of the Pinochet dictatorship in 1973. Barbara Jackman and Nancy Goodman were among them. The lawyers told ICCR members about an important refugee case before the Supreme Court of Canada, the case of *Singh et al*, and said that there was a need for interveners. Given its long-standing role in resettling refugees from overseas in Canada, the CCC appeared to be an appropriate body to intervene. ICCR agreed and the CCC agreed. Barbara Jackman and the then chair of Amnesty International's refugee committee, Michael Schelew, acted as co-counsel.

I remember an issue for the Supreme Court was the question of whether Canadian responsibility extends to what happens overseas. It seemed to us then that the 1951 Convention relating to the status of refugees provided a responsibility link by article 33, *non-refoulement*, the provision prohibiting deportation if life or freedom would be threatened.

This informal introduction to constitutional law was to lead to promoting an understanding of refugee rights in Canadian courts and in international human rights bodies. These activities culminated in my sitting in the Toronto

1

courtroom of the Court of Appeal for Ontario with representatives of Amnesty International's refugee committee in 2001, hearing Barbara Jackman argue the *Ahani* case.

My reflections and experience over the years have led me to see these Canadian cases as a testing of the courts and of the *Canadian Charter of Rights and Freedoms* and their ability to offer non-citizens in Canada the international rights which Canada is obligated to provide.

In this book, I show that it is possible to develop a test for measuring international human rights treaty obligations. My approach uses that test to examine court decisions. I end my examination with great concern for rights of individuals in extradition and deportation. More of this will emerge as the story unfolds.

In 1982, the Constitution was brought home to Canada. A *Canadian Charter of Rights and Freedoms*, subsequently referred to simply as "the *Charter*," was incorporated.[1] It was to serve as the supreme law of Canada. The Supreme Court is the highest court in Canada. It could apply the *Charter* decisively to override any other laws which did not conform with the supreme law. *Charter* rights can in theory "trump" the law.[2] This was the early expectation, and in the early case of *Singh et al* in 1985 the Court did just that. The intervention by the CCC in that case played a significant role. The Court found that those claiming refugee status had a right to at least one hearing in person before the decision maker. The focus was due process. Later, I show

---

[1] Patrick Monohan, *Constitutional Law*, 2nd Ed., Toronto, Irwin Law, 2002, 173-176.
[2] Robert J. Sharpe, Kent Roach, *The Charter of Rights and Freedoms*, 3rd Ed., Toronto: Irwin Law, 2005, 27.

that in this decision the *Charter* rights gave effect to international rights which Canada had promised.

In the words of the principal UN treaties, everyone under Canada's jurisdiction is to benefit from the international human rights treaties that Canada has ratified. Courts are to protect individuals from acts of the authorities that might violate their fundamental rights. In 1984 Canada's Ambassador Beesley assured the UN Human Rights Committee (HRC), that:

> "although the *Charter* [*Canadian Charter of Rights and Freedoms*] and the Covenant [Covenant on Civil and Political Rights, CCPR[3]] were not identical ... differences could not hide the high degree of similarity ... The *Charter* gave effect to many of Canada's obligations under the Covenant."[4]

Bayefsky's 1992 book conveys this expectation from that time. Van Ert's 2002 book repeats that the *Charter's* drafters drew on the CCPR.[5] Sharpe and Roach agree that the *Charter* was "influenced by these international developments."[6] Since 1985 a gap has grown between the Courts' rulings on rights matters for non-citizens and the international human right obligations as confirmed by the views of the committees that are built into the human rights treaties, the "treaty bodies."

---

[3] Covenant on Civil and Political Rights, CCPR, December 19, 1966, Can. T.S. 1976 No. 47

[4] Anne F. Bayefsky, *International Human Rights Law: Use in Canadian Charter of Rights and Freedoms Litigation*, Butterworths, Toronto/Vancouver, 1992, 54.

[5] Gibran Van Ert, *Using International Law in Canadian Courts*, The Hague: Kluwer Law International, 2002, 238.

[6] Sharpe and Roach, *Op.Cit.* 2005, 15.

Before 1991, UN treaties clearly obligated Canada to protect individuals from deportation when a risk of torture or cruel treatment was a foreseeable consequence. They obligated Canada to prevent deportation when separation of children from parents was a foreseeable consequence. In 1990 when Canada joined the Organization of American States, OAS, additional obligations required Canada to ensure fair trial rights in the adjudication of such important substantive rights. However, in 1991 there was little case law or jurisprudence from human rights treaty bodies to confirm how the treaty obligations apply to non-citizens and their deportation or extradition.

This book will explore the gap as it relates to non-citizens, to deportation and to extradition (a) because there has been growth in both Canadian court and international human rights jurisprudence, (b) because the area is inherently international as I will explain, and (c) because this is the area of my personal experience. The focus will be on the treaty obligations themselves - what the treaty words require – and then what the courts did. I will comment on, but not delve into, the current interest in the courts and their use of international law.

Changes in Law and a Swing from Singh

To almost all those who had testified in prior parliamentary hearings, the revisions to the *Immigration Act* which came into force in January 1989 did not appear to satisfy *Charter* rights. I recall that the explicit expectation of the parliamentarians at the time was that the courts could use the *Charter* to correct any oversights made in legislation.[7] So when the changes came into effect, the Canadian Council of Churches, with the support of other non governmental groups (NGOs), took all the offending provisions of the *Immigration Act* before the Supreme Court and asked the Court to strike down these offending parts of the legislation. The CCC and the ICCR were well situated to take the lead in this broadly supported NGO initiative and felt some obligation to do this, having successfully intervened in the case of *Singh et al.*

Central among the concerns was ensuring that everyone claiming refugee status be given a fair hearing and a meaningful appeal before they could be expelled from Canada. Other key concerns included protecting from torture and protecting family and children's rights in forms of expulsion. Further concerns were powers in the *Immigration Act* which seemed close to arbitrary powers for detention. There were also concerns about excessive powers for search and seizure and about excessive penalties for helping refugees arrive without required documentation. Then in 1992, the Supreme Court dismissed the Council of Churches' case on grounds that the Council did not have "standing" to raise a case on behalf of refugees.

A gap between the promise of *Charter* rights for non-citizens and the reality was soon noticed. In 1995 Pearl Eliadis described a marked shift after 1985 in the Supreme Court's decisions relating to non-citizens as a "Swing from Singh."[8] But Eliadis did not explore this as a gap between

---

[7] I was present alongside other NGOs for almost every session of House committee and Senate committee hearings on then Bills C55 and C84.

[8] Pearl Eliadis, "The Swing from Singh: The Narrowing Application of The Charter in Immigration Law.", 26 Imm. L.R. (2d) 130, 1995.

the *Charter* case law and international human rights law. She also did not take into account the intervening application of the *Charter* in extradition situations which this essay shows to be relevant.

Since Eliadis, many others have reviewed the role of international rights in the extradition and deportation cases of the courts that will be examined here. However, they have not done so on a detailed case-by-case basis, and they have not taken an international obligations perspective. For example, Gerald Heckman examined the increasing references to international rights and the generally lowered procedural safeguards the Supreme Court has provided for non citizens.[9] Thomas Bateman examined the extradition cases and international rights with a "two tensions" theory.[10] Many scholars have written about important individual court decisions, in particular the *Baker* and *Suresh* decisions. This book uses the international obligations as a basis for examining these Canadian law cases.

Concern for International Obligations

Beginning in the early 1980s, the World Council of Churches (WCC) began to convene periodic global meetings of national member churches around refugee issues. As a consequence, understanding of the international nature of the movement of refugees grew. When one country deported, another country had to

---

9 Gerald P. Heckman, "Securing Procedural Safeguards for Asylum Seekers in Canadian Law: An Expanding Role for International Human Rights Law", 15 IJRL 212.

10 Thomas M.J. Bateman, "The New Globalization in Canadian Charter of Rights Interpretation: Extradition, the Death Penalty, and the Courts," 7 International J. Human Rights 49, 2003.

receive. This was not a local legal issue, but an international matter. It called for international standards which international human rights treaties appeared to promise. To the extent that the international human rights obligations were not reinforced by international human rights case law, it seemed important to facilitate that case law.

Led by a special sense of the international dimension of the question and facing a sense of loss with the failure of the major Canadian Council of Churches' court action initiative in 1992, non governmental groups in Canada began to send cases involving possible human rights violations before the available complaints procedures of the international human rights treaties. This was not coordinated internationally, but Canadian NGOs were aware of parallel efforts in several European countries and in Australia and New Zealand.

Beginning in 1990, the Canadian Council of Churches sent a "report" on Canada to facilitate the UN Human Rights Committee's evaluation of Canada's implementation of the CCPR. That report considered rights of Aboriginal peoples, policing, prison and racial difficulties as well as rights of non-citizens. In 1992, the Council of Churches put the failed omnibus court challenge case as a complaint before the Inter-American Commission on Human Rights and also submitted two individual cases. Other NGOs and lawyers submitted cases as well.

The Canadian Council of Churches had led popular fundraising across the country with concerned NGOs in order to finance the court challenge of the 1989 immigration legislation. When the challenge was ended in 1992, the Council held residual funds in trust. Also the Council had been promised some matching funds by the then Court Challenges Program of the federal government. The Council was successful in having these promised federal funds put into trust when that program was closed. Thus the Council of Churches found itself with two funds held in trust, one internal and one external, which could be applied to pay legal costs to litigate legal issues raised by the original court challenge.

The Canadian Council of Churches set up a joint committee with the Inter-Church Committee for Refugees to disburse these two funds. Largely through word of mouth in the NGO community, lawyers applied for funding at Ontario legal aid rates to prepare cases in Canada and before international human rights treaty bodies which would raise the issues that had been raised in the failed court challenge. Almost all the interventions before the Supreme Court in the cases described in this book were financed in this way. The *Baker* case was special as will be seen. The Canadian Council of Churches, the Canadian Council for Refugees, and others were able to appear before the Inter-American Commission in a General Hearing in Washington in the fall of 1996 and to participate in a subsequent on-site visit of the Commission to Canada in 1997. The visit led to a report with advice in 2000. [11]

The result of NGO action in Canada and elsewhere in the world, was to facilitate the emergence of some of the international jurisprudence which has at the time of writing largely confirmed the views of the NGOs and scholars about the obligations.

---

[11] Inter-American Commission on Human Rights, "Report on the Situation of Human Rights of Asylum Seekers within the Canadian Refugee Determination System', OAS doc. OEA/Ser.L/V/II.106, Doc.40 rev., Feb. 28, 2000, para. 95. ("Inter-American Commission 2000 Report")

Mark Freeman and Gibran Van Ert have published two books in which international human rights obligations and some views of treaty bodies and Canadian Courts are provided and discussed.[12] [13] My book makes the detailed comparison of international obligations with the rulings of Canadian courts on the selected cases. My contribution adds a reflection on rights which recur in international case law about non-citizens, such as the right to freedom of movement, the right to seek and obtain asylum, and a right to a court remedy. I also spend some time considering and quoting from the report of the Inter-American Commission on the status of human rights in Canada's refugee determination system because Freeman and Van Ert did not discuss the implications of this report. I will refer to it as the "Inter-American Commission 2000 Report."

I revisit Freeman and Van Ert's comparisons of the views of the Canadian courts and the views of the international human rights bodies to explore my concern for the cause of the gap for each particular *Charter* right for non-citizen cases and extradition cases.

As testified by Van Ert's 2002 book and the books of Freeman and Van Ert in 2004 and 2005, there is renewed Canadian interest concerning the effect of international human rights treaties in Canadian law. There is also a general awareness of a gap between the views of courts in Canada and the international human rights obligations. For example, in 1999, after the Supreme Court's decision on *Baker*, Craig Scott wrote hopefully about the possible

---

[12] Mark Freeman & Gibran Van Ert, *International Human Rights Law*, Toronto: Irwin Law, 2004.
[13] Mark Freeman & Giran Van Ert, *International Human Rights Law: Texts, Cases, and Materials*, Toronto: Irwin Law, 2005.

closing of the *gap* between jurisprudence relating to rights promised from UN human rights treaties and the implementation of the rights by the Courts in Canada.[14] His work was particularly concerned with economic, social and cultural rights. In a 2000 review of the work of the Supreme Court of Canada, William Schabas noted that the UN human rights treaty committees have sometimes issued different decisions on cases after the Supreme Court has already heard and ruled on them.[15] Schabas used the pertinent non-citizen extradition example of the *Ng* v. *Canada* decision by the UN Human Rights Committee (HRC), acting under Protocol I to CCPR. Most recently, the 2004 book by Freemen and Van Ert discusses aspects of the gap for some substantive rights in some of the cases to which I shall refer.

Jurisprudence, that is, case law, general comments and country-specific advice, from the international human rights bodies has accumulated. Over the years, the various UN treaty bodies have issued comments addressed to Canada following the examination of Canada's human rights reports to them. Selections from these are now available in the book by Freeman and Van Ert.[16] However, the 2000 report by the Inter-American Commission on Human Rights presents specific advice on human rights in Canada's refugee determination system, clarifying Canada's obligations as a member of the Organization of American States. The Commission recommended improvements in the access to courts for non-citizens, a meaningful appeal

---

[14] Craig Scott, " Canada's International Human Rights Obligations and Disadvantaged Members of Society: Finally into the Spotlight?", 10 Constitutional Forum 97, 1999, 104.

[15] William A. Schabas, "Twenty-Five years of Public International Law at the Supreme Court of Canada", 79 Can. Bar Review 174, 2000, 194.

[16] Freemen & Van Ert, *Op.Cit.*, 2005.

for refugee status determination, improvements in protection from torture and in protection of family and children's rights in expulsion, and better court review of the security certificate that can bring mandatory detention and expulsion to a designated non-citizen.

In its report at the end of 2001, the Senate Standing Committee on Human Rights, the Canadian parliamentary body responsible for international human rights, acknowledged in general terms the international advice, the international treaty obligations and the gap between international obligations and Canadian law.[17]

Many authors have commented on the theoretical role of international law in Canadian law in general, and on that role at the Supreme Court of Canada in particular. In 1992, Bayefsky concluded that the Supreme Court invoked international law when it supported a conclusion already reached by the Court, but that international law was otherwise ignored.[18] In 2001, Stephen Toope confirmed that the Supreme Court's use of even the more specific international human rights law remained uncertain.[19] In his 2002 book, Van Ert confirms this conclusion for international human rights law.[20]

Several broad themes emerged in a debate renewed in 2001-2002 among scholars about the role of international law: the principle of self government versus the role of a

---

[17] "Promises to Keep: Implementing Canada's Human Rights Obligations", Report of the Standing Senate Committee on human Rights, December 2001, 8.

[18] Bayefsky, *Op. Cit.* 1992, 95.

[19] Stephen Toope, "Use of the Metaphor: International Law and the Supreme Court of Canada", 80 Canadian Bar Review, 534, 2001, 538-539.

[20] Van Ert, *Op.Cit.*, 2002, 252.

treaty as source of law; whether international treaties are to be applied by the courts in a more principled way as binding on Canada; and whether special forms of customary international law are to be given effect by courts in Canada. In an earlier paper than his book, Van Ert summarized the use of treaties by Canadian courts.[21] He noted two principles: "the rule that treaties must be implemented by statute in order to alter domestic law" and "statutes should be construed consistent with the presumption the legislature does not intend to violate international law." These two principles are elaborated for human rights treaties in his book of 2002.[22] These appear expanded into four pillars in chapters of his later book with Freeman.[23]

Karen Knop took the view that international law and human rights law is material to be "translated" by national courts in the manner developed in comparative law.[24] Jutta Brunnee and Stephen Toope make a case that the courts have an obligation to interpret domestic norms in conformity with binding international norms.[25]

The principled approach of Brunnee and Toope appeals to a layman's notion that obligations under the ratified human rights treaties should have greater significance in Canadian law than other international human rights law. Knop's

---

[21] Gibran Van Ert, "Using Treaties in Canadian Courts," 38 Canadian Yearbook of International Law 3, 2001, 16 & 28.

[22] Van Ert, *Op.Cit.*, *2002,* Chapter 7.

[23] Freeman & Van Ert, *Op.Cit.* , 2004, Chapters 8 and 9.

[24] Karen Knop, "Here and There: International Law in Domestic Courts", 32 New York University Journal of International Law and Politics 501, 2000.

[25] Jutta Brunnee and Stephen J. Toope, "A hesitant Embrace: The Application of International Law by Canadian Courts", 40 Canadian Yearbook of International Law 3, 2002.

notion of "translation" of international law seems particularly relevant in the context of interpreting the limits to be set on rights. Yet without a principled framework for translation, a court could do what Bayefsky described in her 1992 book – pick and choose from international case law to support a decision already made.

A distinction can be made between how human rights treaties should affect *Charter* rights as compared with how international law in general affects a law in Canada.[26] This distinction is stated by Gibran Van Ert:

> "There is a sense in which human rights treaties do not establish new obligations but merely declare the 'inherent,' 'self-evident' or 'universal' rights of humanity. ... the doctrine of universality is unquestionably a rule of international law ... The universality of human rights imports special considerations for Canadian courts and counsel working with international human rights treaties."[27] [28]

Van Ert goes on in his later 2002 book to suggest:

> "Universality means that international human rights instruments are properly of interest to Canadian courts independent of their bindingness ... as attempts to express a conception of personhood to which Canada has committed itself domestically." [29]

---

[26] Bayefsky, *Op.Cit.*, 1992, 95 and 126.
[27] Gibran van Ert, *Op.Cit.*, 2001, 79-85.
[28] See further in Freeman & Van Ert, *Op.Cit.*, 2004, 24, 37, 175-178.
[29] Van Ert, *Op.Cit.*, 2002, 234.

All these authors say little about some specifics of concern to this book – how the international treaty obligations to give effect to and to ensure CCPR rights apply to a court and to the *Charter*. The cases examined in this book are ones in which the *Charter*, if interpreted by a court to be compatible with international human rights obligations, would require the court to make changes in legislation like the *Immigration Act, 1976*.

For the layman, Brunnee and Toope's "presumption of conformity with international law" in the context of CCPR rights, should require a court to use the *Charter* so as to give effect to a CCPR right. A possibility of the courts using the *Charter* to give effect to international rights has been acknowledged. Professor Peter Hogg notes in his standard textbook on the Canadian Constitution that there is a special relationship of the *Charter* with the UN Covenant on Civil and Political Rights, CCPR.[30] He also makes particular reference to the American Declaration of Rights and Duties of Man. On the other hand, most recently, Freeman and Van Ert state:

> "One area of continued uncertainty ... is the reception of international human rights law through the *Charter*. Apart from some specific comments on the relevance of international law in interpreting the *Charter* sections 1 and 7 ... the Supreme Court ... has so far failed to elaborate a satisfactory and consistently applied approach ..."

To sum up, the *Charter* was intended to give effect to CCPR rights but the courts have failed to do that. While Canadian courts have made some references to CCPR treaty rights in

---

[30] Peter W. Hogg, *Constitutional Law of Canada*, Student Edition 2003, Toronto:Thomson Canada, 2003, 734.

the cases considered in this book, they have almost never mentioned the obligations Canada has with respect to the American Declaration of Rights and Duties of Man. As we shall see, the *Charter* could give effect to American Declaration rights, even though this was not initially intended by the framers of the *Charter*. The Declaration became binding on Canada after the *Charter* came into force.

For me and seemingly for Freeman and Van Ert, a court should act on Canada's obligations to give effect to international treaty human rights through the application of the *Charter*. This is not established.[31] In their reasoning, Freeman and Van Ert accept the general principle that the international treaty human rights should prevail unless there is some explicit legislative intent to the contrary. But what if an interpretation of the *Charter* giving effect to international human rights treaty obligations would conflict with a particular law? A supreme law like the *Charter* relies on a broader form of democratic legitimacy than the single federal or provincial election providing legitimacy for a particular law like the *Immigration and Refugee Protection Act, 2002*. To me, this means that an international right given effect by the *Charter* should trump Canadian law just as the *Charter* can trump Canadian law.

Exploring the Gap

That there is a gap between Canadian court positions and international human rights case law positions is beyond dispute. It is equally clear that the gap involves some

---

[31] These authors see great merit in the "Slaight" approach but show the court has also taken a very different approach. See Freeman & Van Ert, *Op.Cit.* 2004, 189-193.

ambiguity in the role of the *Charter* in giving effect to international human rights. For an international observer, and for this book, that begs another question. At the end of the day, can Canadian courts be relied upon to live up to Canada's obligations to "ensure" and to "give effect" to CCPR and other key international treaty human rights. Are further legal measures required of Canada? If so, what?

This book's exploration involves considering the courts' application of the *Charter*. David Beatty's general review of constitutional law acknowledged that for some areas of law the Supreme Court has avoided enforcing the supremacy of the supreme law.[32] Beatty noted that other nations' Constitutional Courts have acted similarly with areas of their law.[33] He noted that a series of consistent and reasoned decisions is already an achievement. A reasoned decision in an evolving coherent body of law is better than nothing. But a reasoned decision is not enough to meet the obligation to ensure the international rights of an individual before a court.

Monahan has supported the Supreme Court's shift away from a role of appeal court for the individual criminal towards that of a reviewer and shaper of the law in general.[34] In part contrast, Peter Hogg viewed the *Charter* itself as ultimately directed at respect for individual liberty, dignity and privacy.[35] Monahan has also reinforced a powerful conceptualization of Hogg and Bushell that the Court's judicial review role is part of a "dialogue" between

[32] David Beatty, *Constitutional Law in Theory and Practice*, Toronto, Buffalo, London: University of Toronto Press, 1995, 85-95.
[33] *Ibid*, 105.
[34] Patrick J. Monohan, "The Supreme Court of Canada in the 21st Century", 80 Canadian Bar Review 374, 2001, 378.
[35] Hogg, *Op.Cit.* 2003, 726.

the Court and the legislature.[36] The Supreme Court has itself acknowledged this dialogue metaphor.[37] Clearly, shaping a body of law and dialogue with the legislature are valuable. But they are distinct from the obligation to ensure the international treaty rights to life and to protection from torture for an individual non-citizen, and to ensure rights to fair trial and access to courts. For me, ensuring the individual's rights must take precedence.

There are now some factors pushing the Supreme Court towards upholding international human rights obligations. Among others, Stephen Toope has implied a form of dialogue between the Supreme Court and the international treaty bodies.[38] Today's nation State is part of a community of States in which one State's law is part of a wider pool of international community law.[39] Yet given the established court practices and the newer factors which this book considers, the question is whether the Canadian courts can be expected to ensure international treaty human rights for vulnerable non citizens such as those who are accused of being security risks and who face the violation of fundamental rights such as the right to protection from torture in expulsion.

The Outline of the Book

This book explores the gap in a particular way. Returning to first principles, it sets out the texts of international human rights treaty obligations. It examines their implications for a court as opposed to a government or a legislature. It develops an international obligation test

---

[36] Monahan, *Op.Cit.* 2001 , 388; Monahan, *Op.Cit.* 2002, 404.
[37] *Vriend* v. *Alberta,* [1998] 1 SCR 493, para. 137-139.
[38] Toope, *Op.Cit.* 539.
[39] Toope, *Ibid.*

against which to measure court decisions. The body of the essay then uses this test for a comparison of the Supreme Courts' non-citizen and extradition case law with the closely corresponding international human rights case law. That comparison is made on cases set out in chronological order to follow the evolution of the Canadian and the corresponding international human rights case law. The absence of references to academic reflection is in part my attempt to approach the cases in a new way through the optic of an international obligation test. I return to the text of a court decision itself and look at that from the vantage point of the authoritative international advice about the human rights obligations.

In chapter 2, we shall consider the nature of the pertinent international human rights obligations. We shall develop a test from the underlying key obligations. They will be reinforced by general and specific advice from international human rights treaty bodies about the application of the treaty rights. We shall look at the implementing provisions in Canadian law.

The successive chapters 3 - 5 follow a historical sequence of the evolution of the gap in the selected cases. I have chosen to break the case law into groups in time somewhat arbitrarily to better reveal correspondence with the evolution of international human rights case law. Thus, for example, the cases Singh and Andrews in chapter 3 are in a period before the 1990 examination of Canada before the UN Human Rights Committee and I summarize the relevant international case law as it was at the end of that period.

The swing from Singh in chapter 4 established a wide deviation from international standards for extradition and expulsion, and during this same period a range of specific corresponding international human rights jurisprudence and case law was generated. I have chosen to mark the end of this period with the March 1999 examination of Canada by the Human Rights Committee.

The cases of *Pushpanathan* and *Baker* discussed in chapter 5 gave the Supreme Court some chance to close the gap. Interestingly, the UN Human Rights Committee's 1999 examination of Canada was prior to the Supreme Court decision on *Baker*. In it, the HRC gave specific advice with respect to family rights that were at issue in the *Baker* case. In both its *Pushpanathan* and *Baker* decisions the Supreme Court gave some effect to some international rights, but did not close the gap.

In 2000, just prior to the final period considered, UN advice was complemented by a thorough report with recommendations by the Inter-American Commission on Human Rights about human rights obligations and Canada's refugee determination system. Chapter 6 begins at the beginning of the 21st century, when the Supreme Court had an opportunity to revisit extradition and expulsion following the Inter-American Commission 2000 Report in the cases of Burns and Suresh respectively in 2001 and 2002.

As this book was to go to press, the Supreme Court heard an appeal by other individuals. According to the Canadian Broadcasting Commission report on the internet, 13 June 2006, Mohamed Harkat, Adil Charkaoui and Hassan Almrei had all been held for years in jail because Canadian Security Intelligence Service alleged they had ties to al-Qaeda terrorists. The security certificate procedures allowed the authorities to detain foreign-born nationals indefinitely without charge and without making public any evidence against them. The decisions on these cases could modify my conclusions with respect to one relevant international right, CCPR article 9(4), and the corresponding *Charter s. 10 Habeas Corpus*. However, it would be difficult for the Court to address the accumulated gaps with several international rights which it has developed over the years.

Throughout the chapters I offer insights into the work of the Canadian churches and other NGOs in Canada concerned about the human rights of refugees and non-citizens. I also insert occasional personal reflections on pertinent themes such as the legitimacy of deportation.

The final chapter follows in time the examinations of Canada by the UN Committee against Torture in May 2005 and by the UN Human Rights Committee in October 2005. It reviews the gap from the perspective of the obligation on a State like Canada to take the necessary steps to give effect to international treaty rights and hence to close the gap. It reviews the potential of the *Charter* to give effect to international treaty rights and of the courts, left to themselves. It concludes that additional legislative changes are necessary and suggests some.

2. International Obligations and the Court

The Obligations and a Test

The starting place for considering a Canadian court's relationship to international human rights obligations is the obligations themselves. They arise from the human rights treaties that Canada has ratified such as the UN Covenant on Civil and Political Rights.[40] These have built into them the formation of a committee that has functions with respect to the treaty. One obligation is that the ratifying State, Canada, must provide a report on its implementation of the treaty periodically for the committee to examine. The committee will question the State on its report and will then issue a "Report" on the examination with recommendations to that State. The committee may also issue "General Comments" for all the States about the implementation of the treaty rights. For States like Canada that have specifically agreed, the committee may receive complaints from individuals after the individuals have exhausted legal avenues available in the State. The committee will then give "views" on the complaint (referred to as a Communication) and whether or not one or more of the individual's treaty rights have been violated.

All three functions of the treaty committee are built into the CCPR taken together with Optional Protocol I. The views and the general comments are in some sense part of the treaty and to my mind form a context in which treaty

---

[40] I use the names used in comments and views of the treaty bodies for the treaties, omitting the prefix "International" often used in academic texts and sometimes adding the prefix "UN" to distinguish UN and OAS for the layman. I distinguish international case law by adding "HRC" for the UN Human Rights Committee and "IACHR" for the Inter-American Commission on Human Rights.

provisions are to be interpreted under the 1969 Vienna Convention on the Law of Treaties.[41] From an international perspective, a particular provision of the treaty, a particular "right" like the right to life, is to be interpreted in this context of the treaty as a whole. The treaty as a whole certainly includes the treaty bodies and it must include in some way their views. At the same time the views were not intended to be judgments – hence the very term "views." Nonetheless, these views and comments by human rights treaty bodies are unique and authoritative. As the UK put it:

> "The UK is of course aware that the General Comments adopted by the Committee are not legally binding. They nevertheless command great respect ..."[42]

Similar arrangements to those creating a committee under the CCPR apply to the UN Convention against Torture and Other Cruel, Inhuman or Degrading Treatment or Punishment, CAT,[43] and the UN Convention on the Rights of the Child, CRC.[44]

A treaty Canada has entered into and is said to be "binding" on Canada. The treaty body's opinion as to how the treaty applies is said to be advisory and non-binding. However, the precise meaning of the treaty can sometimes be ambiguous, and in an international situation like extradition or deportation of a non-citizen, there is no other

---

[41] Vienna Convention on the Law of Treaties, 1969, [1980] C.T.S./R.T.C. 37; 1155 U.N.T.S./R.T.N.U. 331; (1969) 63 A.J.I.L. 875

[42] Observations by the United Kingdom on General Comment No. 24, 16 HRLJ 424, 1995.

[43] Convention Against Torture and Other Cruel, Inhuman, or Degrading Treatment or Punishment, U.N. doc. A/RES/39/46, 10 December 1984.

[44] Convention on the Rights of the Child, 1989, 1577 U.N.T.S. 3.

equally compelling evidence that a national court might draw on about the interpretation of a somewhat ambiguous obligation than the views of the treaty body. Academics like Hathaway may be critical of the case law of a treaty body with respect to refugees and asylum seekers.[45] NGOs and academics may be unhappy about members of a treaty body – sometimes with cause.[46] Governments may have good cause to object to the view of a treaty body about an issue such as their reservations.[47] Individual members of a committee may have different views from the majority. Nonetheless, the majority decision of a treaty body stands as the best available international perspective on the precise meaning of the treaty obligation. It is worth adding that the General Comments and the Report (or concluding observations) directed at Canada are adopted by consensus of the treaty body. While the International Court of Justice has authority to rule on such matters, until some government or qualified body takes an issue before the ICJ, a unique international source for evidence is the international human rights body. Hence this book relies on such authority and gives less weight to the views of academics or national judges or justices with respect to the obligations in a treaty. Local authorities do not enjoy the international status of the treaty body as a whole - appointed by States Parties in accordance with the formal nomination and election procedures and established by the provisions of the treaty.

---

[45] James C. Hathaway, *The Rights of Refugees under International Law,* Cambridge: Cambridge University Press, 2005, 131-144.

[46] Dinah Shelton, "Memorandum of Concern on the Elections of Officials to Committees and the Organs of the Organization of American States," 14 HRLJ 454, 1993.

[47] Observations by he United States of America on General Comment No. 24 (52), 16 HRLJ 422, 1995; Observations by the United Kingdom on General Comment No. 24, 16 HRLJ 424, 1995.

There need be no concern that using the treaty body interpretations might in some way limit or restrict rights in Canada. First, this book reveals that for non-citizens Canadian courts have been at least as rights restrictive as the treaty bodies. Secondly, CCPR Art.5 requires a non-restrictive interpretation of the CCPR. Nothing in the CCPR can be used to justify restrictions on CCPR rights to any greater extent than the CCPR provides for. The CCPR cannot be used to restrict any other rights otherwise promised by a State Party. If a court or legislature granted rights beyond the CCPR these would not be restricted by the CCPR.

Canada attracted additional human rights obligations by joining the Organization of American States, OAS. The very act of joining required adherence to the American Declaration of Rights and Duties of Man and recognition of the Inter-American Commission on Human Rights as the mandated authority to promote these rights. Freeman and Van Ert take the view, which I share, that the American Declaration of Rights and Duties of Man is best treated as if it were a ratified treaty.[48] Since the views of the Inter-American Commission have been less used in Canada, more information is warranted here.

The Inter-American Commission on Human Rights is an autonomous organ of the Organization of American States, OAS, created to protect and promote the observance and defense of human rights and to serve as a consultative body of the OAS. The seven members of the Commission are elected by the General Assembly of the OAS for four-year terms. They serve as individuals to represent all the member countries of the OAS. The authority of the Commission stems from a combination of

---

[48] Freeman & Van Ert, *Op.Cit.*, 2004, 216.

the OAS Charter, the American Convention on Human Rights, the American Declaration of the Rights and Duties of Man, its Statute and its Regulations. These instruments define the human rights of the peoples of the Americas under international law and provide mechanisms for their protection. The Commission can issue study reports, receive individual complaints alleging violations of rights and give advice to member States to further their observance of human rights. [49]

For interpreting the treaties and the obligations they impose, the 1969 Vienna Convention on the Law of Treaties sets the standards.[50] Article 31 requires using the ordinary meaning of the text of a provision of a treaty in the context of the whole treaty. It also requires using the juridical context of subsequent formal agreements. States that ratify the OAS Charter attract obligations under the OAS Charter and the American Declaration of Rights and Duties of Man.[51] The authority of the Inter-American Commission on Human Rights with respect to the OAS Charter and the American Declaration stems from a combination of its mandate and the Statute and Regulations subsequently approved by the OAS. Thus the jurisprudence of the treaty committees and the Commission is unique and authoritative for the specific

---

[49] Organization of American States, *"Basic Documents Pertaining to Human Rights in the Inter-American System"*, OAS Doc. OEA/Ser.L./V/I.4 re.8, 22 May 2001, 10, 119, 123.

[50] Schabas, *Op.Cit.* 2001,179, Freedman & Van Ert, *Op.Cit.* 2004, 55.

[51] "... in preparing the present report, the Commission has interpreted Canada's obligations in relation to the OAS Charter generally, and the American Declaration more specifically. Pursuant to general principles of interpretation, other relevant rules of international law applicable to Canada must be taken into account in construing its regional human rights obligations. ..." Inter-American Commission 2000 Report, *Op.Cit.*, para. 38.

provisions of the treaty in question. All human rights treaties are to be interpreted in this current juridical context.[52]

The CCPR is particularly relevant because, like the *Charter*, the CCPR is focused on civil and political rights. Its special relationship with the *Charter* stems in part from the common declared derivation from the inherent dignity of the human person and the concept of universality.[53] [54]

The Inter-American Commission on Human Rights has a special authority within the OAS system: it can interpret the range of human rights treaties for OAS member

---

[52] "... An international instrument has to be interpreted and applied within the framework of the entire legal system prevailing at the time of interpretation ...", *Legal Consequences for State of the Continued Presence of South Africa in Namibia (South West Africa) Notwithstanding Security Council Resolution 276 (1970)*, Advisory Opinion, ICJ Reports, 1971, at 16 paragraph 53; "... Treaties that affect human rights cannot be applied in such a manner as to constitute a denial of human rights as understood at the time of their application...", *Gabcikovo-Nagymaros Project (Hungary/Slovakia)*, Judgment, ICJ Reports 1997, at 7 paragraphs 114; "... to determine the legal status of the American Declaration it is appropriate to look to the inter-American system of today in the light of the evolution it has undergone since the adoption of the Declaration, rather than to examine the normative value and significance which that instrument was believed to have had in 1948", *Interpretation of the American Declaration of the Rights and Duties of Man within the Framework of Article 64 of the American Convention on Human Rights*", Advisory Opinion OC10/89, Inter-American Court of Human Rights, July 14, 1989, at paragraph 37; "... the Convention is a living instrument which ... must be interpreted in the light of present day conditions", *Tyler* v. *U.K.*, Judgment, European Court of Human Rights, Series A, No. 26, 25 April 1978, at Paragraph 31.
[53] Van Ert, *Op.Cit.* 2001, 80.
[54] Hogg, *Op.Cit.* 2003, 734.

States.[55] In its 2000 Report on Canada, the Inter-American Commission used this authority to interpret UN human rights treaties to advise Canada on further implementation of international rights, advising not just on rights promised in the American Declaration, but on rights in the CCPR, CAT and Convention on the Rights of the Child as these relate to corresponding OAS Charter and American Declaration rights. According to the reasoning of Brunnee and Toope, the American Declaration should be binding on Canada when the provisions are clear obligations of the "shall" kind. Within the Inter-American Commission 2000 Report, the government of Canada is reported as acknowledging the American Declaration as a source of obligations.

The reports of the Inter-American Commission and the opinions and judgments of the Inter-American Court are

---

[55] As noted in broad terms above, this authority to interpret treaties stems in part from its mandate under American Convention article 41 to promote progressive human rights among the States of the region, and in part from it role in presenting cases before the Inter American Court of Human Rights – a Court which has the authority to interpret human rights treaties in the Americas. The IA Commission was questioned on the matter of other treaties by Canada in its Report on Human Rights in the Canadian Refugee Determination System (See *Op. Cit. para 38*). The Commission replied in part quoting the Inter American Court (Advisory Opinion OC-1/82 of September 24, 1982 "Other Treaties...", Ser.A No 1, para 43: "The Commission has properly invoked in some of its reports and resolutions 'other treaties concerning the protection of human rights in the American states', regardless of their bilateral character or whether they have been adopted within the framework or under the auspices of the inter-American system". See also IA Court, Advisory Opinion OC 14/94 of December 9th 1994 "...Laws in Violation of the Convention" Ser.A No 14 para 25, 28 making reference to the Commission mandate in American Convention art. 41 "to make recommendations ... for the adoption of progressive measures in favour of human rights...".

said to be "non binding." Yet the Commission and Court, by virtue of their status within the OAS system which Canada accepted, offer an authoritative international interpretation of Canada's obligations under the American Declaration. As noted for UN treaty bodies, short of the International Court of Justice, there is no individual or body with comparable international authority to interpret Canada's obligations under the American Declaration – itself binding. The fair trial or due process obligations are strongly stated in the American Declaration and are relevant for several cases considered. Yet these have not been explored fully by Freeman and Van Ert in their 2005 book.[56]

If one wishes to bring an international test to measure the performance of the Canadian Courts with respect to the international rights, the positions taken by the treaty bodies seem the most legitimate source to use, with all the caveats and, sometimes, with my own discomfort about them.

Three general State obligations are set out in the CCPR:

(1) to respect and ensure rights to individuals;
(2) to give effect to rights; and
(3) to ensure an effective remedy for a violation.[57]

These obligations were listed and accepted as obligations by Canada's Standing Senate Committee on Human Rights

---

[56] Freeman & Van Ert, *Op.Cit.* 2004, 275-276.

[57] Under the CCPR the State Party undertakes: art 2.1 "to respect and to ensure to all individuals ... the rights ... in the present Covenant without distinctions of any kind ..."; art. 2.2 "to take the necessary steps ... to adopt such legislative measures or other measures as may be necessary to give effect to the rights recognized in the present Covenant"; art. 2.3 "to ensure that any person whose [CCPR] rights ... are violated shall have an effective remedy ...and to develop the possibility of judicial remedy".

in its 2001 report.[58]

The CCPR text of article 3(a) right to effective remedy anticipates that "persons in an official capacity" might commit a violation. So ensuring an individual's rights or providing an effective remedy cannot logically be carried out by the same or closely related officials to those who might violate a right. A court can play this role, but the CCPR stops short of requiring that. Also, since officials might commit a violation, one might suppose that a case involving the State and involving the possible violation of a CCPR right would be viewed as a suit at law to which article 14.1 should apply.[59] However, the HRC itself has not given full effect to the article 14.1 due process in its case law on CCPR rights in extradition and deportation. In its *Ahani v. Canada* case, the HRC hinted that due process applies within the non-citizens special CCPR Art. 13 right to present reasons against expulsion, but at the same time the HRC failed to give any effect to the CCPR article 14(1) right to an independent and impartial tribunal to adjudicate the right to protection from torture.[60]

On the other hand, the obligations from the American Declaration leave no doubt that for Canada, a member of the OAS, an effective remedy must be judicial.[61] The

---

[58] Standing Senate Committee on Human Rights, *Op. Cit.* 2001, 14.

[59] Manfred Nowak, *UN Covenant on Civil and Political Rights: CCPR Commentary*, NPEngel: Kehl/Strasbourg/Arlington, 1993, 241-243 Para. 9-12.

[60] "The Committee notes that as article 13 speaks directly to the situation in the present case and incorporates notions of due process also reflected in article 14 of the Covenant, it would be inappropriate in terms of the scheme of the Covenant to apply the broader and general provisions of article 14 directly." Human Rights Committee, Views, *Ahani v. Canada*, Communication No. 1051/2002, UN Doc. CCPR/C/80/D/1051/2002 25 May 2004, Para.10.9.

[61] Freeman & Van Ert, *Op.Cit.* 2004, 275.

relevant American Declaration provision, Art. XVIII, states:

> "Every person may resort to the courts to ensure respect for his legal rights ..."

A legal "remedy" must allow every person: "the right to resort to the courts to ensure respect for legal rights" and access to "a simple brief procedure whereby the courts will protect him or her from acts of authority that violate any fundamental constitutional rights."[62] These are clear and binding. The "effective judicial remedy" required here has been further clarified for Canada in several immigration contexts by the Inter-American Commission 2000 Report. It is viewed by the Commission as a "right":

> "The right of access to judicial protection to ensure respect for a legal right requires available and effective recourse for the violation of a right protected under the Declaration or the Constitution of the country concerned."[63]

CCPR article 5, allows a better right, here the American Declaration fair trial right, to prevail in any conflict of rights with CCPR article 2(3) effective remedy. OAS case law interprets this effective judicial remedy as one that is effective for the individual involved in two ways: establishing a violation or not of a right at issue; and, providing redress.[64]

---

[62] Inter-American Commission Report 2000, *Op. Cit.*, para. 95, 96, 98.

[63] Inter-American Commission Report 2000, *Op. Cit.*, para. 95.

[64] "... the absence of an effective remedy to violations of rights recognized by the Convention [here the American Convention on Human Rights] is itself a violation of the Convention ... for such a remedy to exist, it is not sufficient that it be provided for by the Constitution or law ... but rather it must be truly effective in

As we shall see, in the particular circumstances of *Judge* v. *Canada*, the HRC found that a person being deported to a death penalty should have been allowed prior access to an existing court appeal which might have affected his situation.[65] The Committee against Torture noted that, when substantial risk of torture is at issue, a judicial review on the merits is an obligation under the CAT:

> "the State party should provide for judicial review of the merits, rather than simply of the reasonableness, of decisions to expel an individual where there are substantial grounds to believe the person faces a risk of torture." [66]

Despite ambiguity, one can set out a minimal three-part test for a court decision complying with international human rights obligations:

(1) did the court respect and ensure international rights for individuals,
(2) did the court give effect to international rights and
(3) did the court ensure an effective judicial remedy for the individual's rights?

The Supreme Court is the organ of the Canadian State that attracts the obligation to ensure an effective judicial remedy for an individual in a particular situation. Only a court can

---

establishing whether there have been a violation of human rights and in providing redress." Inter-American Court of Human Rights, *Judicial Guarantees in States of Emergency*, Advisory Opinion OC-9/87, October 6, 1987, para. 24.

[65] HRC, *Judge* v. *Canada*, Communication No. 829/1998, Views 20 October 2003, UN Doc. CCPR/C/78/D/829/1998.

[66] Committee against Torture, Conclusions and Recommendations, Canada, CAT/C/CO/34/CAN, May 2005, Para. 5c.

best satisfy the treaty obligation to protect the individual before it from acts of government or the authorities as the CCPR and American Declaration require. Only the Supreme Court can ultimately ensure such a remedy by its oversight of the law. This international obligation must logically be an obligation falling on the appeal courts in general and the Supreme Court in particular.

The Supreme Court is governed by the Supreme Court Act and section 40 gives the Court the scope to carry out Canada's international obligations:

> "(1) Subject to subsection (3), an appeal lies to the Supreme Court from any final or other judgment of the Federal Court of Appeal or of the highest court of final resort in a province ... where ... the Supreme Court is of the opinion that any question involved therein is, by reason of its public importance or the importance of any issue of law or any issue of mixed law and fact involved in that question, one that ought to be decided by the Supreme Court or is, for any other reason, of such a nature or significance as to warrant decision by it, and leave to appeal from that judgment is accordingly granted by the Supreme Court."

According to one of the international authorities, the international understanding of the role of domestic courts with respect to a human rights treaty is:

> "It is generally accepted that domestic law should be interpreted as far as possible in a way which conforms to a State's international legal obligations. Thus, when a domestic decision maker is faced with a choice between an interpretation of domestic law that would place the State in breach of the Covenant

> and one that would enable the State to comply with
> the Covenant, international law requires the choice
> of the latter..." [67]

There is a recent General Comment 31 with more specific
observations by the UN Human Rights Committee:

> " ... The Committee notes that the enjoyment of the
> rights recognized under the Covenant can be
> effectively assured by the judiciary in many
> different ways, including direct applicability of the
> Covenant, application of comparable constitutional
> or other provisions of law, or the interpretive effect
> of the Covenant in the application of national law.[68]

A compatible understanding has been noted in chapter 1
from Canadian authors such as Hogg,[69] Bayefsky,
Schabas,[70] by Brunnee and Toope and by Freeman and Van
Ert.[71] Unless domestic law expressly provides otherwise,
Canadian law should be interpreted so as to conform to
international law.

For most of this essay, the relevant Canadian law is the
supreme law - the Constitution and the *Charter*.[72] The

---

[67] Committee on Economic Social and Cultural Rights, General
Comment No 9 [1998], para. 15, UN Doc. HRI/GEN/1/Rev.6, 12 May
2003, 55.

[68] Human Rights Committee, General Comment No.31[80], Nature of
the General legal Obligation Imposed on States Parties to the Covenant,
UN Doc. CCPR/C/21/Rev.1/Add.13 26 May 2004., para. 15.

[69] Hogg, *Op.Cit.* 2003, 734.

[70] Schabas, *Op.Cit.* 2001,183.

[71] Freeman & Van Ert, *OP.Cit.* 2004, 175-178.

[72] Hogg, *Op.Cit.* 2003, 1173, 1205, 1207. The Canada Act 1982 was
passed by the UK giving effect to the Constitution Act 1982. The
Constitution Act 1982 renamed the former British North America Act

Charter is the principle means whereby CCPR rights might be given effect and ensured. The early expectation was that the *Charter* would be interpreted to conform with CCPR obligations. Under Canadian law, other laws in Canada must conform with the *Charter*. As noted by Freeman and Van Ert cited in chapter 1, this is not now the accepted approach of the Canadian courts.

International Rights and *Charter* Rights

Generalities about giving effect to rights by the *Charter* are one thing, specifics are another. Variations in the details of international rights and Charter rights can make it difficult to fulfill the obligations. In their 2004 book, Freeman and Van Ert recognize this and go into specifics which they discuss as a matter of "reception" for some selected rights including those falling under *Charter s.7* which are relevant for this present book. So I pause here to set out the relevant similarities and differences as I see them. The rights and obligations that this essay will examine relate particularly to forms of expulsion, extradition and deportation, and to forms of detention. Most cases also relate to non-citizens. In earlier joint articles I examined some comparative international human rights case law relating to non-citizens rights and found the following rights had been at issue:

- life;
- liberty;
- protection from torture or cruel treatment;
- freedom of movement
- protection of family life;
- seek and receive asylum; and
- non-discrimination.[73]

1867 as the Constitution Act 1867. The Constitution Act 1982 included a *Canadian Charter of Rights and Freedoms* as Part I.

73 Tom Clark and Sharryn Aiken in collaboration with Barbara

I have recently summarized some of the relevant current comparative international case law relating to non-citizens and to protection from torture and protection of family and liberty.[74] However, for this book the focus is on the particular human rights treaties binding on Canada and the corresponding international interpretation. An obligation does not relate to international case law about a more or less comparable right. It relates to the precise wording of the text of the treaty ratified. Here, then, are the precise obligations (rights) to be respected, given effect and ensured.

Under CCPR article 6, right to life:

> "no one shall be arbitrarily deprived of his life" and "... the death penalty ... may be imposed ... not contrary to the ... Covenant ... and ..."

CCPR article 9, right to liberty and security of person, requires:

> "9(1) Everyone has right to liberty and security of person ..." and,
> "9(4) "Anyone who is deprived of his liberty by arrest or detention shall be entitled to take proceedings before a court, in order that that court

---

Jackman and David Matas, "International Human Rights Law and Legal Remedies in Expulsion: Progress and Some Remaining Problems with Special Reference to Canada", Netherlands Quarterly of Human Rights, Vol. 14, December 1997, 431-437; Tom Clark in collaboration with Francois Crépeau, "Human Rights in Asylum Sharing and Other Human Transfer Agreements," 22 NQHR 217, 2004, 223-226.

74 Tom Clark, "Rights Based Refuge, the Potential of the 1951 Convention and the Need for Authoritative Interpretation", 16 International Journal of Refugee Law 584, 2004.

> may decide without delay on the lawfulness of his
> detention and order his release ..."

The reference to "lawfulness" here goes beyond the national law and can include aspects of international lawfulness.[75]

Note that the CCPR right to life involves aspects of due process relating to the death penalty. Any deprivation cannot be "arbitrary" and the death penalty must be imposed in a matter that conforms with the Covenant. The HRC has confirmed relevant aspects are CCPR article 14 fair criminal trial provisions and the CCPR article 7 protection from torture and cruel treatment. The CCPR right to life with its due process is distinct from the CCPR right to liberty and security of person. The right to liberty and security of person stands alone in CCPR sub article 9(1). The due process relating to a deprivation of liberty in CCPR article 9(4) requires a court. In theory *Charter* s.10 provides that by s.10(c) *Habeas Corpus*:

> "Everyone has the right on arrest or detention
> *a*) to be informed promptly of the reasons therefor;
> *b*) to retain and instruct counsel without delay and
> to be informed of that right; and
> *c*) to have the validity of the detention determined
> by way of *habeas corpus* and to be released if the
> detention is not lawful."

The American Declaration of the Rights and Duties of Man promises in article I:

> "Every human being has the right to life, liberty
> and security of the person."

---

[75] Nowak, *Op.Cit.* 1993, 179-182.

This is a substantive stand-alone right. However, under the American Declaration Art. XVIII:

> "Every person may resort to the courts to ensure respect for his legal rights ..."

Thus, from an international obligation perspective, to give effect to these international rights, Canadian law must be capable of recognizing a substantive right to life, liberty and security of the person as well as two distinct CCPR rights, each with slightly different and distinctive due process components attached.

The *Canadian Charter of Rights and Freedoms* s.7 provides that:

> "Everyone has the right to life, liberty and security of the person and the right not to be deprived thereof except in accordance with the principles of fundamental justice."

This can be read to be consistent with international rights if read in the ordinary meaning of the words to give two distinct components: the right to substantive life, liberty and security of the person; and, the right to the fundamental principles of justice in any deprivation. This reading can allow the right to include both the corresponding CCPR rights with their due process components and the substantive rights in American Declaration of the Rights and Duties of Man Art.I. When the right to life is at issue, "the principles of fundamental justice" would correspond with "in conformity with the CCPR." When the right to liberty is at issue, "the fundamental principles of justice" would correspond with a court decision which can determine the lawfulness of detention and order release. "The fundamental principles of justice" must include access to "the court to ensure respect for" the substantive rights to life, liberty and security of the person.

The Canadian courts have found the meaning of fundamental principles of justice to include substantive and procedural elements[76] and aspects of international law.[77] However, *Charter s.7* as a whole has not been applied so as to ensure or give effect to Canada's corresponding international human rights obligations to life, liberty and security of the person as Freeman and Van Ert imply. They are concerned with the "balancing exercise".[78] In the cases examined, this balancing exercise has undermined the obligation to give effect to and to ensure the international treaty rights set out above.

Under article 7 of the CCPR:

> "no one shall be subjected to torture or to cruel or inhuman or degrading treatment or punishment."

This international right may not be suspended in a time of emergency - in contrast with some other CCPR rights which may be suspended as provided in CCPR article 4. CCPR article 7 is distinct from, but relevant to *Charter s.7*, because the HRC has said it can be an aspect of the death penalty and so an aspect of the deprivation of the right to life.

The Convention against Torture came into force later than the CCPR, elaborating an aspect of CCPR Art. 7. Under the

---

[76] Sharpe and Roach, *Op.Cit.* 2005, 207-208; Freeman and Van Ert, *Op.Cit.* 2004, 255.

[77] Freeman and Van Ert, *Op.Cit.* 2004, 199.

[78] Freeman and Van Ert, *Op.Cit.* 2004, 255-256.

Convention against Torture article 3:

> "No State Party shall expel, return (*refouler*) or extradite a person to another State where there are substantial grounds for believing that he would be in danger of being subjected to torture."

This obligation reinforces a pre-existing obligation of the State under the CCPR: "to ensure" protection from torture. Ensure is a strong obligation. In this case the obligation was to ensure the individual's CCPR Art.7 protection from torture when torture was foreseeable as a consequence of expulsion. The Human Rights Committee views and General Comment 31 are consistent with this interpretation:

> "Moreover, the article 2 obligation requiring that States Parties respect and ensure the Covenant rights for all persons in their territory and all persons under their control entails an obligation not to extradite, deport, expel or otherwise remove a person from their territory, where there are substantial grounds for believing that there is a real risk of irreparable harm, such as that contemplated by articles 6 and 7 of the Covenant, either in the country to which removal is to be effected or in any country to which the person may subsequently be removed." [79]

The *Canadian Charter s.12* requires:

> "no one shall be subjected to cruel or unusual treatment or punishment".

---

[79] Human Rights Committee, General Comment 31, *Op.Cit.*, para.12.

This provision of the *Charter* could be interpreted so as to give effect the international rights. It would then encompass protection from torture as an extreme form of cruel treatment or punishment. Canada has consistently argued before the Committee against Torture that it does.[80] CAT article 16, cruel treatment, implies a lower threshold of concern than torture per se as defined in CAT article 1. The absolute prohibition of torture itself *per se* is not included in the *Charter*.[81] As we shall see, and as Freeman and Van Ert note,[82] the courts have not given effect to CAT Art.3 or the CCPR obligations by *Charter s.12*. In its 2005 Concluding Observations following its examination of Canada, quoted at the end of chapter 6, the Human Rights Committee called upon Canada to live up to this obligation.

CAT articles 3 and 16 present a clear and binding link of this right with expulsion. CCPR article 7 prevention of torture taken with CCPR article 2 (to "ensure" the right) requires the same link. Ensuring a right means ensuring protection of the right consequential to any State action such as expulsion. However, *Charter* s.12 does not refer to expulsion and the *Charter* does not require any court to "give effect to" and "ensure" the rights in it.

The American Declaration on Rights and Duties of Man has no counterpart to CCPR Art.7 prohibition of torture and cruel treatment. American Declaration Art. I has a right to life liberty and security of the person and the Inter-American Commission on Human Rights has used its authority to interpret the right in a current juridical context so as to include protection from torture. The same

---

[80] Freeman and Van Ert, *Op.Cit.* 2004, 279-280.

[81] The definition of torture and some other articles of the Convention against Torture are given some effect by the *Criminal Code*. But this federal law does not enjoy the status of the *Charter*.

[82] *Ibid* 280 -282.

possibility for interpretation is of course open for the right in *Canadian Charter s.7*. However, as Freeman and Van Ert observe, the protection via *Charter s.7* has been weaker in an extradition context.[83]

The CCPR Art.12(2) and 12(4) freedom of movement rights to leave his country and to enter his own country are different from the *Charter*:

> 12 (2) "Everyone shall be free to leave any country, including his own."

This 12(2) right can be limited as provided in 12(3) provided restrictions "are provided in law, necessary to protect national security, public order (ordre public), public health or morals or the rights and freedoms of others and are consistent with the other rights recognized in the present Covenant." Article 12 continues:

> 12(4) "No one shall be arbitrarily deprived of the right to enter his own country."

This wording "his own country" intends to go beyond citizens and to include aliens and stateless persons who have such a strong attachment to the State that it can be viewed as their own country or home country and this can be confirmed by the *traveaux préparatoires*.[84] In contrast, *Charter* s. 6.1 states:

> "Every citizen of Canada has the right to enter, remain in and leave Canada."

---

[83] Freeman and Van Ert, *Op.Cit.* 2004, 281-282.
[84] Nowak, *Op.Cit.* 1993, 219.

The *Charter* limits the right to enter and remain to a citizen of Canada. The CCPR does not. I have suggested elsewhere that the International Court of Justice *Nottebohm Case* shows that there is an international law perspective on nationality which may not coincide with the State assignment of its citizenship.[85] As we shall find, part of the gap with Canadian law in expulsion of *Chiarelli* can be attributed to this distinction.

The American Declaration Art. XXVII provides a right to seek and receive asylum "in accordance with the laws of each country and with international agreements." Note that there is a right of access to a court to ensure respect for all rights under the American Declaration. Moreover, the case law of the Inter-American Commission about the right to seek and receive asylum has quite reasonably determined that the twin components of "laws of each country" and "international agreements" must both be simultaneously satisfied. The 1951 Convention relating to the status of refugees, ratified by Canada, qualifies as one of the international agreements.[86]

The American Declaration obligation with respect to the right to seek and receive asylum is potentially significant. It means that when a Canadian legal procedure offers what is

---

[85] Clark and Aiken, *Op.Cit.* 1997, 436.

[86] Tom Clark with Francois Crepeau, "Mainstreaming Refugee Rights: The 1951 Convention and International Human Rights Law," Netherlands Quarterly of Human Rights, Vol. 17, 389, December 1999, 394. See IACHR *Joseph Case,* Report No.27/93, Case No.11.092, Decision as to admissibility, 6 October 1993, Annual Report of the Inter-American Commission on Human Rights, 1993, at p. 46 Para.31. See also IACHR *Haitian Interdiction Case*, Report No.51/96, Case No.10.675, Decision on Merits, 13 march 1997, Annual Report 1996, at pp. 598-602. See also Inter-American Commission 2000 Report, para. 58-60, 68-70.

in its effect a right to asylum in accordance with "international agreements" such as the 1951 Convention, that right must be also in accordance with the other pertinent international agreements such as the human rights treaties. Further, it means that the right to asylum requires protection by the courts according to the American Declaration. Although the right to asylum is not given effect by the *Charter*, it is given effect in Canadian law by means of the references to the 1951 Convention relating to the status of refugees in the *Immigration and Refugee Protection Act, 2002*.

Ensuring CCPR family rights and children's rights, article 17, 23 and 24 can preclude expulsion:

> "no one shall be subjected to arbitrary or unlawful interference with his privacy, family, home or correspondence ..." and,
> "everyone has the right to the protection of the law against such interference". (CCPR Art. 17)
> "The family ... is entitled to protection by ...the State." (CCPR Art. 23)
> "Every child ... the right to such measures of protection as are required by his status as a minor ..." CCPR (Art. 24)

The American Declaration articles V, VI and VII promise in turn:

> "Every person has the right to the protection of the law against abusive attacks upon his ... family life."
> "Every person has the right to establish a family ... and to receive protection therefore."
> "... all children have the right to special protection, care and aid."

The Convention of the Rights of the Child, CRC, articles 9(1) and 10(1) require in turn:

> "States parties shall ensure that a child shall not be separated from his or her parents against their will except when competent authorities subject to judicial review determine ... that such separation is necessary for the best interests of the child. ..."
>
> "In accordance with ... article 9.1, applications by a child or his or her parents to enter or leave a State Party for ... family reunification shall be dealt with ... in a positive, humane and expeditious manner ..."

The *Charter* makes no explicit protection for the protection of the family and of children's rights that arise in expulsion. However, interveners in the Baker case argued that *Charter* s.7 protection of life, liberty and security of the person could be applied to non-citizens and to any of their children who are citizens. Not to do so places non-citizens and citizens unequally before s.7 of the supreme law. As noted, the American Declaration brings a right to fair trial and access to courts for these substantive family and children's rights.

CCPR Art. 2(1) requires respecting and ensuring all CCPR rights without distinction of any kind:

> "Each State Party ... undertakes to respect and to ensure to all individuals ... the rights recognized in the present Covenant, without distinction of any kind, such as race, colour, sex, language, religion, political or other opinion, national or social origin, property, birth or other status."

CCPR Art. 14(1) is distinct and requires equal treatment before the law, although it is taken alongside CCPR Art. 26 non-discrimination in the jurisprudence.[87] [88] CCPR Art. 26 offers general non discrimination when any right or benefit is offered whether in the CCPR or not. American Declaration Art. II is a right with respect to American Declaration rights:

> "All persons are equal before the law and have the rights and duties established in this Declaration, without distinction as to race, sex, language, creed or any other factor."

The jurisprudence of the HRC indicates a distinct right to equal treatment with respect to the non-citizen's right to give reasons prior to expulsion. The Inter-American Commission 2000 Report makes a similar point about equal treatment before the courts and tribunals.

Charter s.15 (1) states:

> "Every individual is equal before and under the law and has the right to the equal protection and equal benefit of the law without discrimination..."

In theory, *Charter s.15(1)* could give effect to both equal treatment and non-discrimination dimensions of the international treaty rights. As we shall see, this has not yet been the practice for some non-citizens.

---

[87] Nowak, *Op.Cit. 1993*, 240 Para. 8.
[88] Hathaway, *Op.Cit.* 2005, 131-145.

Responsibility of the Court

A court is a relevant State organ that can uphold some of Canada's international human rights obligations. The UN Human Rights Committee has confirmed this evident responsibility of the courts in General Comment 31:

> "The obligations of the Covenant in general and article 2 in particular are binding on every State Party as a whole. All branches of government (executive, legislative and judicial), and other public or governmental authorities, at whatever level - national, regional or local - are in a position to engage the responsibility of the State Party."[89]

The CCPR text in the preamble requires this from anyone in Canada, which would include judges:

> "... the individual ... is under a responsibility to strive for the promotion and observance of the [CCPR] rights."

One way the Court can "give effect" to international rights is by "giving effect" to the corresponding *Charter* rights in a manner compatible with the international rights. The language of the obligations, "give effect" to rights, "respect" rights, and "ensure" rights, speaks to a proactive approach for a Court.

To my mind, when one interprets the *Charter* through the lens of international human rights law, as this book does, the *Charter* in turn requires the Court to "ensure" that the *Charter* is enforced as the supreme law precisely so that the *Charter* can "give effect" to and "ensure" international

---

[89] HRC, General Comment 31, *Op.Cit.*, para. 4.

rights at issue in cases before the Court through corresponding *Charter* rights. However, Canadian law does not require that. The Court has done so. It has not always done so.

Before applying my test to particular case law, this essay pauses to examine briefly possible factors in the *Charter* that might justify the gap between international standards and Canadian law: the *Charter* judicial remedy; the *Charter* limits on rights; and, judicial appointments.

As noted above, CCPR obligations include (a) the CCPR article 14(1) right to equal treatment before courts and tribunals and (b) the CCPR article 14(1) right to an independent and impartial tribunal for the determination of rights in a suit in law.[90] As noted, this latter part of the right is not developed in the HRC non-citizen case law. In contrast, CCPR article 13 clearly applies to non-citizens in expulsion situations. Any expulsion of a non-citizen lawfully in the territory must follow a decision reached in accordance with the law and the non citizen shall be allowed to submit reasons against his or her expulsion. This CCPR article 13 requires aspects of due process and in particular, equal treatment. What remains unclear is exactly what aspects are required beyond equal treatment in access to the CCPR article 13 right.[91]

In addition to the CCPR obligations for due process and for an effective remedy under article 2, the OAS right requires a special kind of due process and judicial remedy. The American Declaration of Rights and Duties of Man[92] Art.

---

[90] Nowak, *Op.Cit.*, 1993, 238-241.

[91] See HRC *Ahani v. Canada, Op.Cit.*, para. 10.9.

[92] Hogg notes this Declaration alongside the CCPR as relevant to the application of the *Canadian Charter* , see Hogg, *Op.Cit.*, 2003, 735.

XVIII states:

> "Every person may resort to the courts to ensure respect for his legal rights. There should likewise be available to him a simple brief procedure whereby the courts will protect him from acts of authority that, to his prejudice, violate any fundamental constitutional rights."

To "ensure respect" for rights (CCPR Art.2) is a strong obligation. If a court is to ensure, the obligation requires a low threshold for access to a court. The American Declaration court remedy must be capable of protecting the individual from the acts of the authorities that violate fundamental rights. Both the CCPR Art.2(3) and the American Declaration court access are international obligations for a court interpreting *Charter* s.24 in Canada. Unfortunately, *Charter* s. 24(1) is weaker than both of the international obligations. It promises:

> "Anyone may apply to a court if any of their *Charter* rights are "infringed or denied."[93]

The individual "may apply," but what then? *Charter s.24* does not say an individual will be heard or that there will be protection for fundamental rights. True, the wording about rights infringed or denied could be made compatible with the CCPR Art.2 wording "violated." Hogg notes that the *Charter* wording about rights that "have been infringed or denied" is interpreted to impose stricter requirements of

---

[93] "Anyone whose rights or freedoms, as guaranteed by this Charter, have been infringed or denied may apply to a court of competent jurisdiction to obtain such remedy as the court considers appropriate and just in the circumstances." *Canadian Charter of Rights and Freedoms*, s. 24.1.

standing, that is, of getting permission to present the case before a court, than are applicable to many remedies under the general law.[94] A tough standing requirement does not seem compatible with ensuring an effective remedy and protecting fundamental rights from the acts of the authorities.

The Supreme Court review is the final point in the Canadian legal scheme at which the right of an individual to an effective judicial remedy could be upheld by an organ of the State. It would be unreasonable to expect the "administrative authorities" to do this, yet, as will be shown, the Supreme Court has found situations compatible with the *Charter* where "the Minister adjudicates fundamental international rights.

Limiting Some Rights

Limits can be set on some rights and these limits are important. Knop notes that "to give effect to rights" is purely mechanical. Yet precisely because it is purely mechanical it should not be a difficult or controversial thing for a court to do routinely. In contrast, the obligation "to ensure" these rights requires judges capable of determining whether the limits on the rights meet a principled test in that situation for that individual often in the context of a politicized public mood. The situation for extradition or deportation or detention of non-citizens will inevitably involve a local situation which Canadian judges are well equipped to assess, but there is always an international dimension. As I will show later, in *Suresh*, the Supreme Court has recognized a Canadian and an international perspective. The Court has set out the rights obligations, but it has not produced a principled test for

---

[94] Hogg, *Op.Cit.*, 2003, 858.

adjudicating the rights at issue as rights. International treaty bodies with all their faults, go beyond a mere setting forth of rights involved in a case. Human rights case law is frequently judging whether limits by the authorities on rights have been legitimate, necessary and proportionate in specific circumstances.[95] Within this framework, international bodies have found flexibility to adjust the outcome while reinforcing a continuing principled approach. I think particularly of the European Court of Human Rights case law relating to the right to protection of family life in expulsion situations. Surprisingly, this has not been the approach of the Supreme Court to the cases we shall examine.

In Canadian law, *Charter* rights can be limited by applying *Charter* s.1. In theory, *Charter* s.1 can be used by a Court to give effect to the international obligations such as the limits in CCPR article 12 freedom of movement or the softer law principles developed by treaty bodies for limiting rights in general.[96] Several international rights may be limited in the binding sense of Brunnee and Toope. For example, CCPR Art.12 right to freedom of movement, particularly relevant for some non-citizens, specifies within the right how this particular right may be limited. The HRC has pointed out that the limit must be proportionate and consistent with other CCPR rights:

> "Article 12, paragraph 3, clearly indicates that it is not sufficient that the restrictions serve the permissible purposes; they must also be necessary to protect them. Restrictive measures must conform to the principle of proportionality; they must be appropriate to achieve their protective function; they must be the least

---

[95] Beatty, *Op.Cit. 1995*, 17.
[96] Schabas, *Op.Cit. 2000*, 188.

intrusive instrument amongst those, which might achieve the desired result; and they must be proportionate to the interest to be protected."

"The principle of proportionality has to be respected not only in the law that frames the restrictions, but also by the administrative and judicial authorities in applying the law. States should ensure that any proceedings relating to the exercise or restriction of these rights are expeditious and that reasons for the application of restrictive measures are provided." [97]

For freedom of movement, CCPR Art. 12(3) is a binding test for limiting that right. As noted, the CCPR Art. 26 right to non-discrimination applies in the granting of any right or benefit. I noted elsewhere that the doctrine for limiting CCPR Art.26 non-discrimination is similar to the doctrine established for the right to freedom of movement.[98] The CCPR Art. 26 test is not binding, but an authoritative interpretation of the treaty from the body established for the purpose. I regard this as "compelling," meaning more that just any "soft law", the term within the framework of Brunnee and Toope's 2002 paper cited in chapter 1. One can combine these two broadly similar tests for a limit on a right, the binding and the compelling, into a single rough general international test for a limit on any right that it is permitted to limit. A broad general test of a limit is:

Is the limit   (1) in law for a legitimate purpose,
              (2) necessary, and
              (3) proportionate or reasonable for the

---

[97] UN Human Rights Committee, "General Comment 27, Freedom of Movement (Art. 12)", UN Doc. CCPR/C/21/Rev.1/Add.9, (1999), para. 24,15.

[98] Tom Clark with Jan Niessen, "Equality Rights and Non-Citizens in Europe and North America", 14 NQHR 245, 1996, 251.

purpose in the context of a human rights treaty? [99]

The Supreme Court applied *Charter* s.1 in its own *Oakes* test[100] so as to give effect to test for a permitted limitation of international rights. However, the formal limitation of rights by *Charter* s.1 has not always been the approach used in the cases reviewed in this book.

Independence of Judges

The independence of the judges is an additional international obligation from the CCPR Art.14.1 right to fair trial. It requires an "independent and impartial" tribunal. In Canada, judicial appointments are by "Order in Council". In the period covered by this essay, the process was essentially that the Prime Minister's office advised the Governor General on appointments -- and so controlled them.[101] So long as no significant fraction of judges retires over a short period, the influence of the government by means of appointment will be slow and indirect. However, during the cases to be examined in this essay, there was a significant retirement of judges.[102]

---

[99] The argument here repeats that developed by: Clark with Crépeau, "Mainstreaming Refugee Rights ...", 17 NQHR 389, 2004, 391, 393; and, Clark, "Rights Based Refuge ...", 16 IJRL 584, 2004, 590-591.

[100] The *Oakes* test may be summarized: (1) sufficiently important objective to justify limiting a right, and (2) reasonable and justifiable in that the measures are proportionate - that is: a) fair not arbitrary; b) designed to achieve the objective; c) rationally connected to the objective. See *R* v. *Oaks* [1986] 1 S.C.R. 103.

[101] Peter McCormick, *Supreme at Last: The Evolution of the Supreme Court of Canada*, Toronto: James Lorimer & Company Ltd., 2000, 175.

[102] "By the end of the Dickson Court, there had been a turnover in the Court's membership; only Lamer ... and Wilson (who would leave within two years) had more than five years of experience." *Ibid*, 26-27.

In his book McCormick said "...[I] see no reason to suggest that prime ministers in general have shown a tendency to stack the court ..."[103] Contrary to McCormick's view, a plausible hypothesis for the change in direction which Eliadis' described as a "Swing from *Singh*" might be new judicial appointments. As noted in chapter 1 and will be shown in chapter 3, there were a large number of new judges. However, we shall find that the early deviation of the Supreme Court from the international standards was before the majority of these new appointments. Appointments alone cannot account for the full change.

---

[103] *Ibid*, 176.

3. Early Charter Days

As I have suggested in chapter 1, the general position taken on the *Charter* when it came into force in 1982 was that it would give effect to CCPR rights. In these ember days of the so called "just society" era of Prime Minister Trudeau, Chief Justice Brian Dickson led a pioneer court that established rules for working with the new *Charter*. There were a number of key decisions. Among these cases are *Singh et al* in 1985 and *Andrews* in 1989 which had a significant impact on the lives of refugees and landed immigrants respectively in Canada. A lesser know case that shaped a major deviation of the Court from international rights standards was the extradition case of *Schmidt* that occurred in this early period.

Singh 1985

Each of the persons in this case claimed refugee status as defined in s. 2(1) of the then *Immigration Act 1976*. The Minister of Employment and Immigration, acting on the advice of the Refugee Status Advisory Committee, made determinations under s. 45 of the Act that none was a Convention refugee. Each then applied for a redetermination of the refugee claim by the Immigration Appeal Board according to s. 70 of the Act. In accordance with s. 71(1) of the Act, the Immigration Appeal Board refused to allow any of these applications to proceed because it did not believe that there were "reasonable grounds to believe that a claim could, upon the hearing of the application, be established." Each applicant then sought judicial review of the Board's decision following s. 28 of the *Federal Court Act*. These applications were denied by the Federal Court of Appeal.

Six of the persons in *Singh et al* were citizens of India who claimed refugee status on the basis of their fear of persecution by Indian authorities if returned to India. The fear was as a result of their political activities and beliefs relating to their association with the Akali Dal party. The seventh, was a citizen of Guyana of Indian extraction who feared persecution on racial, religious and political grounds.

International rights at issue were: CCPR Art. 6 and 9, life liberty and security of person; CCPR Art. 2(3) effective remedy; CCPR Art. 14(1) and 26 equal treatment and non-discrimination. Looking back now we might note that the American Declaration Art. XXVII right to seek and receive asylum was at issue. At the time, the American Declaration was not binding.

Key issues for the Supreme Court were whether the forced return of refugee claimants engaged *Charter* s.7 and whether compliance with the *Charter* required more protections than provided by the *Immigration Act*:

> "The [Supreme] Court considered whether the procedures for the adjudication of refugee status claims set out in the *Immigration Act* violate s.7 of the *Canadian Charter of Rights and Freedoms* and s.2(e) of the *Canadian Bill of Rights*."[104]

The Canadian Council of Churches was allowed to intervene. It argued mainly on the first issue and against an earlier ruling that protection of *Charter* s.7 cannot apply to what another government does after a person has been

---

[104] *Singh et al* v. *M.E.I.*, [1985] 1 S.C.R. 177, 179.

returned to its jurisdiction.[105] The Council argued:

> "... there is a legal and causal connection between a finding that a person is a Convention Refugee through the refugee status determination process and the particular situation in the person's home country which have led him to fear deprivation of life liberty and security of person in that country. This legal and causal link is the protection from *refoulement* or no forcible return. ... it is this link guaranteeing protection that attracts the application of Section 7 of the *Charter*."[106]

Human rights treaty bodies now recognize such a link so that the State that expels when the foreseeable consequence is the violation of an important right by another country is itself accountable for violating that right for the person deported.[107]

The Council of Churches repeated that substantive rights, life, liberty and security of the person, were at issue and that the principles of fundamental justice of *Charter* s.7 required compliance in all essential respects with the rules of natural justice, including an oral hearing.[108] The separation of substantive rights from due process helped the Court make an interpretation of *Charter* s.7 compatible with international rights obligations.

---

[105] Canadian Council of Churches, *Intervenor's Factum, Singh et al,* 1984, para. 52-53.

[106] *Ibid* para.62.

[107] HRC, *Ng* v. *Canada*, Communication No 449/1991, UN Doc. CCPR/C/49/D/469/1991 (1994) para. 14.1.

[108] *Ibid* para.81.

In making its case the Council of Churches distinguished refugees from other non-citizens.[109] The Council also compared the return of a refugee with extradition, remarking that the lower Courts had accepted the possible application of *Charter* s.7 to extradition.[110] The Court moved away from the *Singh* interpretation in its subsequent *Schmidt* case on extradition so that the link with extradition became a liability for refugees. Making a special case for refugees was of doubtful value. The Council later argued that international rights to protection from torture and to protection of family and children's rights apply to everyone in deportation or extradition.

The Court largely accepted the arguments of the Council of Churches. Justice Beetz listed substantive rights at issue:

> "... an accurate summary of the legal rights given to Convention refugees in Canada by the Immigration Act ... right to remain in Canada ... the right not to be removed to a country where life or freedom may be threatened ... if removed ... the right to re-enter if a safe country cannot be found ... the right to be considered under the criteria provided ... for employment authorization ..."[111]

Justice Wilson noted the right to freedom and, in particular, that the right to security of the person would be impaired by a threat of return to persecution:

> "Even if one accepts the narrow approach ... by the counsel for the Minister, 'security of person' must encompass freedom from the threat of physical

---

[109] *Ibid* para.73.
[110] *Ibid* para.74.
[111] *Singh et al, Op.Cit.*, Beetz j., para 11.

> punishment or suffering as well as freedom from
> such punishment itself. ... a ... refugee has the right
> ... not to be removed from Canada to a country
> where his life or freedom would be threatened .. In
> my view, the denial of such a right must amount to
> a deprivation of security of person within the
> meaning of s. 7." [112]

Chapter 2 noted that *Charter* s.7, which Justice Wilson
determined was engaged, reads as a combination of
substantive rights and due process: "Everyone has the right
to life, liberty and security of the person _and_ the right not
to be deprived thereof except in accordance with the
principles of fundamental justice." The corresponding
CCPR rights are distinct: CCPR Art.6 right to life; CCPR
Art.9 right to liberty and security of person. The American
Declaration of Rights and Duties of Man, Art. I, promises
substantive rights to life liberty and security of the person
and the Declaration requires a fair trial hearing for the
adjudication of these substantive rights. *Charter s.7* was
interpreted so as to give effect to the international rights in
Singh and so was the Bill of Rights. *Canadian Bill of Rights*
s.2e should be engaged to require a "fair hearing" whenever
a right or obligation is determined in federal law:

> "Every law of Canada shall ... be so construed and
> applied as not to abrogate, abridge or infringe ... any
> of the rights or freedoms herein recognized and
> declared, and in particular, no law of Canada shall
> be construed or applied so as to ... (*e*) deprive a
> person of the right to a fair hearing in accordance
> with the principles of fundamental justice for the
> determination of his rights and obligations."

---

[112] *Ibid*, Wilson j., para. 93.

Setting out the *Charter* rights involved was essential to "give effect" to and to "ensure" the corresponding international rights at issue. *Bill of Rights s.2(e)* paves the way for the obligation of the American Declaration that there be a court for ensuring respect for a right. At this time, a tribunal, the IAB could adjudicate the rights, with subsequent judicial review on points of law from a court with leave

Having listed the substantive rights, the judges moved to the related due process in *Charter* s. 7 and *Bill* s.2e. The Court considered whether *Singh et al* had the right to a fair hearing and whether the right to that fair hearing required an oral hearing before the decision-maker:

> "If 'the right to life liberty and security of person' is properly construed as relating only to matters such as death, physical liberty and physical punishment, it would seem on the surface at least that these are matters of such fundamental importance that procedural fairness would invariably require an oral hearing ... where a serious issue of credibility is involved, fundamental justice requires that credibility be determined on the basis of an oral hearing ..." ...

> "What the Board has before it is a determination by the Minister based in part on information and policies to which the applicant has no means of access that the applicant for redetermination is not a Convention refugee. The applicant is entitled to submit whatever relevant material he wishes to the Board, but he still faces the hurdle of having to establish ... that on the balance of probabilities the Minister was wrong. Moreover, he must do this without any knowledge of the Minister's case

beyond the rudimentary reasons which the Minister has decided to give him in rejecting his claim. It is this aspect ... I find impossible to reconcile with the requirements of 'fundamental justice' ...".[113]

"Accordingly, the process of determining and redetermining appellants' refugee claims involves the determination of rights and obligations for which the appellants have, under s.2.e of the Canadian bill of Rights the right to a fair hearing in accordance with the principles of fundamental justice."[114]

Interpreting *Charter* s.7 to best conform with the international treaty obligations, the substantive and due process components must be treated as distinct rights as they were in *Singh*. *Bill of Rights* s.2e points in the same direction because it is an independent due process right for federal laws. *Bill of Rights* s.2(e) remains in force for Federal legislation[115] and in theory has on-going significance for the *Immigration and Refugee Protection Act 2002*.

The American Declaration right to seek and receive asylum in accordance with national and international law was tacitly at issue in the Singh et al case. The 1951 Convention in the then *Immigration Act* gave effect to the right to seek and receive asylum and this right attracted international fair trial obligations which were given effect by the Court from the *Bill of Rights* and the *Charter*.

---

[113] *Ibid*, Wilson j., paras. 104-105, 107.
[114] *Ibid*, Beetz j. , para 17.
[115] Hogg, *OpC.it. 2003*, 697, 698.

Commentators have blamed the *Canadian Charter* and *Singh et al* for new costly refugee procedures.[116] Yet the ruling was based on the *Bill of Rights* as well as the *Charter*. Half the judges based their decision on the *Charter*,[117] half on the *Bill*.[118] Both groups found that due process was necessary and that an oral hearing was required. Due process was central to this case decision and due process was seen as a clear and distinct part of *Charter* s. 7. The Court pointed out that the *Bill of Rights* remains part of the Constitution. It reinforced the due process need and this *Charter* interpretation. The Court required no new refugee determination system. It simply required that a refused refugee be given access as of right to the Immigration Appeal Board.

The Court's *Charter* reasoning in the Singh case followed a principled approach: 1) what rights are at issue? Listing them gives them some effect. 2) are they impaired or violated? 3) how can the right be ensured and an effective judicial remedy ensured? 4) does that call for due process and does the due process for these rights require an oral hearing? 5) given so, does *Charter* s.1 nonetheless allow the

---

[116] "Even non-citizens stepping off an airplane onto Canadian soil are entitled to the Charter's protections, an early decision of the Supreme Court that pushed Ottawa to spend hundreds of millions of dollars for a refugee-determination system now seen as a world model." Globe and Mail, Editorial, 20 April 2002.

[117]*Ibid*, Wilson j. at para 79, "The substance of the appellants' case ... is that they did not have a fair opportunity to present their refugee status claims or to know the case they had to meet ..." , and at para. 81, "Everyone in [Canadian Charter] s.7 ... includes every human being who is physically present in Canada and by virtue of such presence amenable to Canadian law."

[118] *Ibid.*, Beetz j. at para. 7, "The main issue ... is whether the procedures followed ... for ... refugee status are in conflict with the Canadian Bill of Rights and ... s.2.e thereof.

government to limit the rights?[119] At the time of *Singh et al*, the Court had not developed its *Oakes* test which could limit rights in accordance with international standards. So the limiting of rights was less principled. The Minister argued that the refugee process was common in other countries and that the Immigration Appeal Board was under strain from the volume of cases so that an oral hearing in every case would be an unreasonable burden on the Board's resources.[120] The Court said the issue was not whether the procedures set out in the Act were reasonable, but whether it is reasonable to deprive the right to life, liberty and security of person by a system that does not conform to the principles of fundamental justice.[121] On limiting rights, the Court concluded with a more rhetorical statement than the principles that emerged later in the *Oakes* test:

> "Certainly, the guarantees of the Charter would be illusory if they could be ignored because it was administratively convenient to do so. No doubt considerable time and money can be saved by adopting ... procedures which ignore the principles of fundamental justice, but such an argument ... misses the point of the exercise under [Charter] s. 1".[122]

Note that at this point, the Supreme Court held that the principles of fundamental justice implied standards of due process rather than a gathering of factors or values. In

---

[119] *Canadian Charter* s.1 reads that the rights and freedoms are guaranteed "subject only to such reasonable limits prescribed by law as can be demonstrably justified in a free and democratic society".

[120] *Ibid* para. 114.

[121] *Ibid* para. 115.

[122] *Ibid* para. 116.

providing "redress", the Court struck down a section of the *Immigration Act* that required leave or permission in order to have an appeal before the then Immigration Appeal Board.

Giving effect to rights and ensuring rights are crucial parts of the international obligations test. In *Singh,* Justice Beetz listed as a "right" the application for a work authorization under administrative law, implicitly giving effect to the international right to work.[123] This giving effect to rights involved as rights is missing in later decisions like *Baker.* Justice Beetz also noted that there must be "at least" one full oral hearing leaving the possibility of leave to appeal after one oral hearing, provided the burden on the applicant to show the probability of success is compatible with natural justice. Access to judicial review became more restricted by the legislative changes of January 1989. The question of the adequacy of appeals and Beetz's concern returned in the Inter American Commission on Human Rights 2000 Report.

The Court respected and ensured the rights of individuals. It gave implicit effect to a range of international rights. It pronounced a violation of due process rights. It created a fair trial hearing by striking out a word in the law. The court ensured a judicial remedy by sending the individuals to the fair trial hearing it created – an oral hearing that was followed by the possibility of judicial review, if by leave on points of law. The weakness around how to determine limits on rights would become more of a problem in the case of *Schmidt.* As will become clear, if the court does not painstakingly give effect to the international rights and give effect to the international limits, the shape of the law may become erratic and the individual may have uncertain

---

[123] Covenant on Economic Social and Cultural Rights, Art. 6-7.

protection for fundamental rights.

Eliadis noted that "*Singh* made it clear that Crown prerogative in this, as in most areas of government action became subject to the rights and fundamental freedoms enshrined in the *Charter*" and that "*Singh* was not an isolated example of a liberal approach to *Charter* interpretation in immigration cases at the time."[124] That is precisely what the American Declaration of Rights and Duties of Man requires under article XVIII. Thus this "liberal approach" can be more objectively described as nothing more than an approach conforming to international human rights obligations.

There is no doubt that the government set out to change this situation and, as we shall see, there can be no doubt that it succeeded. The courts played a part in the success. April 5 1985, Jeff Shallot reported in the Globe and Mail:

> "Immigration Minister Flora MacDonald said she has ordered her officials to comply with the decision and find new procedures for weeding out those who falsely say they are refugees."

> "Mr. Stern [chairman of the Refugee Status Advisory Committee] said the court decision will create some problems and perhaps add to delays in clearing up the backlog of refugee cases."

There had been problems with backlogs of numbers appealing to the Immigration Appeal Board since the 1967 Act establishing it, and authors usually attributed the problems to claims with no merits going before the court.[125]

---

[124] Eliardis, *Op.Cit. 1995*, 131, 132.
[125] Ninette Kelley and Michael Trebilcock, *The Making of the Mosaic:*

Yet the Supreme Court did decide in *Singh et al* that the control valve for getting access to a hearing, the leave provision applied by the Immigration Appeal Board, was unfair to refugee claimants. The Court found this even though many of us at the time did not feel that the cases *Singh et al* were unambiguous refugee cases or persons in dire need of protection. If a right to seek and receive asylum is offered, it must be fairly adjudicated seems to have been the court's approach. The spirit of the *Singh et al* judgment was that upholding rights will cost money and that the money should be found. I add that a State signing a treaty promising to "take the necessary measures" to give effect to and to ensure the CCPR rights, has given an undertaking to pay the costs if that becomes necessary.

It is not clear to me whether the government promoted public hostility towards refugees or merely allowed it to happen. Public hostility towards groups of non-citizens can only have facilitated the subsequent restrictions of their rights by both the federal parliament and, less directly, by a Supreme Court stocked with new justices. Suffice it to say that the noble words of the judgment in *Singh et al* that rights may not be limited for "mere administrative convenience" would not be repeated by the Court in a new context. There was strong anti-refugee and anti criminal public opinion. [126]

The "weeding out" referred to by Flora MacDonald would be applied to those legislated into immigration classifications - classes legislated for non-citizen criminals and non-citizen security risks. The Supreme Court would play a role in facilitating the "weeding out" by

---

A history of Canadian Immigration policy, Toronto/Buffalo/London: University of Toronto Press, 1998, 369-371.
[126] Kelly and Trebilcock, *Op.Cit. 1998*, 417.

misinterpreting the *Charter*. But first, the Court began to pull back in another area.

Schmidt 1987

Unbeknownst to most non governmental actors of that time, the Schmidt case would provide the launching pad for a new interpretation of the *Charter* that would allow Flora MacDonald and the government to accomplish their wish. At the time, extradition from Canada was a two stage process. A judge determined whether the foreign State had sufficient evidence that the person committed an extraditable offense. If so, the Minister of Justice decided whether to surrender the person to the requesting State. (Since 1999 there has been a preliminary step of going before the Minister before going before a judge.) In effect, the law requires a Minister, who has an interest in facilitating his government's extradition to a powerful State like the US, to protect the individual from action of the authorities that may violate fundamental rights – the action is extradition. If there is an effective judicial remedy here, it must lie in the judicial review of that Ministerial decision by the Federal Court or before a provincial appeal court. In this case, the international rights were CCPR Art.9 liberty, Art.12 freedom of movement, CCPR Art.14(7) not to be tried again for the same crime and CCPR Art.2(3) an effective remedy. The American Declaration was not in force, but Art. XVIII would have required court adjudication for substantive rights.

In the courts in Canada, *Charter* s.6 freedom of movement was acknowledged as at issue in the Ministerial decision. At both levels of court *Charter s. 7* liberty was at issue.[127]

---

[127] Hogg, *Op.Cit.2003*, 722.

Schmidt was a Canadian citizen to be extradited to the US accused of kidnapping a 2-year old child from Cleveland. Schmidt was to be sent to the US to face criminal charges that had already been dealt with. She argued she faced the "double jeopardy" that *Charter* s.11 aims to protect against. The Court essentially found that an extradition treaty with the US had more weight than this *Charter* s.11 right.[128] Here is the reluctance of the Court to apply the Supreme Law that Beatty spoke about in his book, as I reported in chapter 1. Hogg put it more gently but more tellingly: "[the Court] not relishing the idea of Canada becoming a safe haven for foreign criminals, has generally been reluctant to interfere with extradition orders."[129] To the lay observer, the concerns displayed in the newspapers had reached the Court, and Hogg is describing a form of political convenience as a factor in the Court's decision-making.

The Court, led by Justice LaForest, moved towards a new test that would later lead to interpretation of *Charter* s.7 in a manner less compatible with international human rights obligations. The majority of judges ignored the distinct substantive and due process rights of *Charter* s.7 identified in the Singh case – the right to life liberty and security of the person <u>and</u> the right not to be deprived thereof except by a procedure that conforms to the fundamental principles of justice.

Chapter 2 showed that *Charter* s.7 has substantive rights and due process rights when applied to give effect to international treaty rights. The due process compnent can be given some effect by the application of *Canadian Bill of*

---

[128] Ed Morgan, "in the Penal Colony: Internationalism and the Canadian Constitution", 49 U. Toronto Law J. 447, 1999, 451-452.
[129] Hogg, *Op.Cit.* 2003, 773.

Rights s.2(e) as in *Singh*. The limits on the rights could follow the international test for limits on international rights involved by the application of *Charter s.1.* Here the Court ignored the *Charter* s.1 *Oakes* test for determining a justifiable limit on both the substantive right to liberty and security at issue and also for determining any limit to the right to a fair trial.

A new test for applying *Charter* s.7 appeared almost in passing as Justice LaForest wrestled with the application of the *Charter*: whether the Court would breach the principles of fundamental justice by extraditing Susan Schmidt to a country where she would be treated in a fashion that "shocks the conscience".[130] Of course this test was not contemplated in a context of consequential death or torture. However, it replaced the Court's obligation to protect the rights of the person with a new test which implied that a court might use the public mood to determine the person's fate – a point subsequently made by dissenting Justice Sopinka in *Kindler* below. To my mind, there is no doubt that public mood is a factor in a court's decision making. That was repeatedly a view of the lawyers representing most of the persons involved in this book. Judges are human. Judges in a court required to protect the individual will be more inclined to seek principled ways to apply the law so as to counter a public mood of the moment. Public mood has little place in a rights based legal system.

Little sense of the obligation to *ensure* international rights and to *give effect* to international rights, including ensuring the right to an effective judicial remedy, comes through in this decision as the judges evidently struggled. The majority failed to see the significance of the consequences of

---

[130] *Canada v. Schmidt*, [1987] 1 S.C.R. 500, 522.

extradition for the rights this book suggests they were obligated to ensure - unless there was a situation where torture would result. It seems the extradition decision was considered just a hearing and not a "fair trial" to adjudicate a treaty or *Charter* right because another jurisdiction, the U.S., provided a trial after extradition. The *Charter* was to apply, but the executive had to have some leeway. It was not clear to the Court that Canada itself had any obligations to ensure a right if Canada was not to be carrying out the trial consequential to the extradition.

Despite the supposed supremacy of the *Charter*, the majority accepted that the executive, in deciding whether to extradite the person, may adjudicate rights such as the right to liberty and the right to freedom of movement. Even before the obligations of the American Declaration of Rights and Duties of Man, the CCPR obligation required an effective remedy that by its nature could protect an individual from acts of authority that might violate any rights, including substantive rights, at issue. I fail to see how a Minister's decision can possible qualify as such an "effective remedy."

The international obligations were not explicitly named in the proceedings but they were somewhat captured in the dissenting opinion of Justice Wilson:

> "This Court held in *Singh* ... that the deportation of any person in Canada (let alone a Canadian citizen) to a country where his or her life, liberty or security of the person was threatened would constitute a violation of s. 7 if the deportation order was not made in accordance with the principles of fundamental justice. It is clear from *Singh* that it is the process in Canada which must comply with fundamental justice. ... *Charter* rights which are

enshrined in our Constitution as part of the supreme law of Canada must be recognized and given effect in any judicial proceeding in Canada unless a reasonable limit justified under s. 1 has been imposed upon them." [131]

However, in the end, it seems Judge Wilson did not feel the need to push her point. She evidently still followed the *Singh et al* notion that the principles of fundamental justice included due process in Canada adequate to ensure the rights at issue. Wilson j. agreed with the outcome. In order to have *Charter* s.7 prevent detention in Canada for extradition, Susan Schmidt needed to show Wilson j. that there would be double jeopardy – that the charge she now faced was the same as the charge from which she had been acquitted previously. It seems she failed to convince Wilson j. of that.

The case record reveals a Court still committed to the *Charter* as supreme law, but concerned about how to relate the new *Charter* to earlier case law on extradition. To my mind, the Court confused the connection between the extradition decision in Canada and the foreseeable consequences elsewhere. The obligation to ensure rights here and now in that context was not understood. The subsequent case law was to build on this confusion.

In the later case of *USA* v. *Controni* Ed Morgan noted "LaForest championed the force of [extradition] treaties over the rights of Canadians under *Charter* s.6.1 [freedom of movement]."[132] Again in this case, Wilson j. again dissented saying that the *Charter* s.6(1), right to life in the

---

[131] *Ibid* 531-533.
[132] Morgan, *Op.Cit. 1999*, 455.

supreme law can preclude extradition. [133] However, for the layman, the issue is not so much the rights of Canadian citizens to freedom of movement, but the more fundamental right of everyone, citizens or non-citizens, to resort to a court to adjudicate fundamental rights and to appeal to a court when an act of the authorities, including a Minister, may violate a fundamental right.

As we shall see later, many were surprised by the later case of *Kindler* when the Court ruled that Kindler could be surrendered by Canada to face the death penalty in the US. A clearer use of the international rights at issue would have helped the court distinguish the cases. In *Kindler* the CCPR Art. 6 right to life was at issue. In *Schmidt*, the CCPR Art. 9 right to liberty and security of person was at issue. The damage was begun by failing to appreciate the strength of the word "ensure" in the obligation to ensure international rights, including the right to an effective remedy for those international rights which in the context must be judicial. That reasoning traces back to the misunderstandings in the Schmidt decision.

Although the Council of Churches had noticed the relevance of extradition to deportation of refugees in passing in its intervention in *Singh et al*, the importance of pursuing this connection was not appreciated. Moreover, the Council of Churches and other NGOs had little stomach for associating themselves with cases of accused criminals that had little seeming relevance to the cause of refugee rights. To raise funds from a broad base of church people to finance legal costs required a focus on refugee needs for fair procedures, protection of life and freedom and promotion of family unity. This unwillingness to become associated with less attractive case situations, though understandable,

---

[133] *Ibid*, 459.

meant there were few interveners present when the Court allowed the law to inadvertently limit international rights in ways that persisted into more attractive cases for church support like the *Baker* case.

Andrews 1989

The case *Andrews v. Law Society (BC)* in 1989 deserves revisiting. At the time, the Canadian Council of Churches and other NGOs working with refugees saw the decision as positive. With hindsight, it is an important transitional case in the emerging gap. The "weeding out" of certain groups that Flora MacDonald spoke of after the Singh et al decision, required making distinctions. *Andrews* is a case about making distinctions on the basis of citizenship under the governance of *Charter* s.15 non-discrimination. Andrews was a non-citizen lawyer who wanted to practice in BC. The Law Society said only citizens could practice. The Court found, I think sensibly, that while some sensitive government legal work might reasonably be for citizens only, there was no reason to deny Andrews from practicing law.

When one applies the international obligations yardstick from the luxurious vantage point of hindsight, the outcome of the Court's judgment seems less positive. The Supreme Court did not give full effect to the international human right CCPR Art.26 by its interpretation of *Charter* s.15. In an earlier paper I showed how under international human rights law doctrine for equal treatment and non-discrimination, similarly situated persons should be similarly treated and any distinction must be in law, for legitimate purpose, necessary and proportionate.[134] For Andrews, the outcome does not change when the

---

[134] Clark with Niessen, *Op.Cit. 1996*, 251.

international test is applied to the distinction between citizens and permanent residents for his right to work in the legal profession.

Beatty, interpreting the *Charter* without reference to international human rights law, described the deviation from the general principles of necessity and proportionality as a "misunderstanding of the [Charter] equality clause" by the Court.[135] The application of the *Charter* following the general principles of necessity and proportionality, also found in international human rights law, would have led to the same outcome.

That people should be equal before the law when claiming a right is a fundamental principle.[136] It is not necessarily at odds with an affirmative action approach. In many situations, similarly situated non-citizens should be treated equally. For example, two persons applying to remain in Canada on humanitarian grounds on the basis of family ties should be treated in the same way if they have substantially the same number of similar family members in Canada. That such persons may not be treated equally when international rights are being adjudicated was part of the complaint in the *Joseph* v. *Canada* case, which lost on admissibility grounds before the Inter-American

---

[135] Beatty, *Op.Cit. 1995*, 94.

[136] CCPR Art.14(1): "All persons shall be equal before the courts and tribunals. In the determination of and criminal charge against him or of his rights and obligations in any suit of law, everyone shall be entitled to a fair and public hearing by a competent, independent and impartial tribunal established by law ...". CCPR Art. 26: "All persons are equal before the law and are entitled without any discrimination to the equal protection of the law ...". American Declaration of the Rights and Duties of Man Art 2: "All persons are equal before the law and have the rights and duties established in this declaration without distinction as to race, sex, language, creed or any other factor."

Commission on Human Rights.[137] Not giving effect to the international right and its doctrine undermined such equal treatment when the circumstances required it. Instead, the Supreme Court approach is based on the different approach to non-discrimination begun in the *Andrews* decision:

> "Discrimination is a distinction which, whether intentional or not but based on grounds relating to personal characteristics of the individual or group, has an effect which imposes disadvantages not imposed upon others or which withholds or limits access to advantages available to other members of society. Distinctions based on personal characteristics attributed to an individual solely on the basis of association with a group will rarely escape the charge of discrimination, while those based on an individual's merits and capacities will rarely be so classed."[138]

This formulation essentially remains. It was built upon and refined into the 3-step test in the later *Laws* decision:

> "First, does the impugned law (a) draw a formal distinction between the claimant and others on the basis of one or more personal characteristics, or (b) fail to take into account the claimant's already disadvantaged position within Canadian society resulting in substantively differential treatment between the claimant and others on the basis of one or more personal characteristics? If so, there is differential treatment for the purpose of s. 15(1).

---

[137] Inter-American Commission on Human Rights, *Joseph v. Canada,* Annual Report 1993, Report No. 27/93, Section VI.
[138] *Andrews v. Law Society of BC, Op. Cit.* 1989, pp. 174-175.

> Second, was the claimant subject to differential treatment on the basis of one or more of the enumerated and analogous grounds? And third, does the differential treatment discriminate in a substantive sense, bringing into play the <u>purpose</u> of s. 15(1) of the *Charter* in remedying such ills as prejudice, stereotyping, and historical disadvantage?"[139]

These formulations depend on persuading the Court that one's personal characteristics impose disadvantages. For me, that judgment can just as easily become a matter of political convenience as deciding whether persons are "similarly situated" as in other formulations. For example, from an international perspective, aboriginal peoples, Roma, migrants, and asylum seekers qualify as disadvantaged groups.

The development of an advanced and nuanced case law relating to non-discrimination for women and homosexuals is regarded as one of the successes of the Supreme Court for the period since 1985.[140] In 1998, in *Vriend v. Alberta,* the court went so far as to read into Alberta's *Individual Rights Protection Act* equal treatment for homosexuals even though the Alberta legislature had expressly omitted such a possibility.

However, the same cannot be said for ensuring equal treatment when important rights of a non-citizen are being adjudicated. The Court of Ontario for Appeal interpreted the Supreme Court's Andrews case as against similar treatment for similarly situated non citizens in its own *Pacificador* extradition case:

---

[139] *Laws v. M.E.I.*, *Op.Cit.*, 1999, para. 39.
[140] McCormick, *Op.Cit.*, 2000, 151-153.

"The appellant [Pacificador] reaches into s.7 of the *Charter* [Canadian Charter of Rights and Freedoms] for an equality right which is not tied to the concept of discrimination. He submits that it is a principle of fundamental justice that all persons must be treated equally before the law, except to the extent that distinctions in their treatment can be justified by some reasonable or rational legislative policy. The concept of equality based on unjustifiable distinctions is not new. It was accepted in the British Columbia court of Appeal in [*Andrews* v. *Law Society of British Columbia* (1986) at 178-182] and applied to a claim made under s. 15. The Supreme Court of Canada however, specifically rejected that approach to equality in the context of s.15.". [141]

I suppose Pacificador might have argued that because the *Charter s.6* right to enter Canada is limited to citizens alone, non-citizens in extradition proceedings are a disadvantaged group who require special safeguards for any fundamental rights at issue. We shall never know. Equal treatment was not forthcoming.

In its views in *Ahani* v *Canada,* the HRC found that the Supreme Court's own different treatment of non citizen Ahani as compared with non citizen Suresh to be in violation of his right to equal treatment with respect to his CCPR article 13 right, the right to present reasons against expulsion. The Court's missing of the international concept of equal treatment in Ahani goes back to its approach to non-discrimination in *Andrews*.

---

[141] *Philippines (Republic)* v. *Pacificador* (1993), 14 OR No.3, 29 July 1993, 321, 336.

This approach, begun in *Andrews* and subsequently developed in case law, failed to question the wide discretion in administrative decisions – precisely the kind of discretion that can say yes to Suresh and no to Ahani facing risk of torture in similar circumstances. Administrative decisions, moderated only by limited judicial review, govern important rights of non citizens under the *Immigration and Refugee Protection Act 2002* and *Extradition Act*. Thus the approach of the Supreme Court in *Andrews* paved the way for weeding out groups of asylum seekers as Flora MacDonald had promised. Indirectly, *Andrews* permits this.

From an international perspective, this approach by the Court in *Andrews* can be viewed both in a positive light as advancing permanent resident non-citizens' work rights. It can be seen in a negative light as a Supreme Court negligent in its duty. The Court was an organ of the State supposed to take the measures necessary to give effect to and to ensure the binding international rights about equal treatment and non-discrimination for everyone in Canada. In part result, some non-citizens remain more equal than others and equal treatment between non-citizens remains lacking in granting rights and benefits relating to entering Canada and expulsion.

Summary of International Advice at 1990

To provide insights into the link between international rights advice and Court rulings in I summarize the available international rights advice here.

Bayefsky reported the 1984 examination of Canada before the UN Human Rights Committee in which Canada's Ambassador Beesley assured the Committee, that "although the *Charter* and the Covenant were not identical ... differences could not hide the high degree of similarity ... The Charter gave effect to many of Canada's obligations under the Covenant."[142] This preceded the decision on Singh et al.

As of 1990, there were relatively few complaints by individual non-citizens in the case law of the UN Human Rights Committee. CCPR article 13, the right to submit reasons against expulsion, aimed at preventing arbitrary expulsion. It applied if non- citizens were lawfully in the territory. The HRC *Maroufidou v. Sweden* case showed that article 13 applied when a State had issued its own documentation, that it had to be in accordance with the law and the law had to be compatible with the CCPR and its non-discrimination provisions.[143] There was similar reference to article 13 and the beginnings of reflection about article 9(1) and detention in *V.M.R.B. v. Canada*.[144] In the somewhat later case of *Giry v. Dominican Republic*, the HRC clarified that article 13, the non-citizens right to present reasons against his or her expulsion, applied to all forms of expulsion, including extradition.[145] Article 13 is a right which, later, Canada would be found to have violated in the 2003 *Ahani* case.

The Committee again found in the case of *Hammel v. Madagascar* that the CCPR article 13 required an expulsion case be reviewed by the competent authorities within a reasonable time. Here, CCPR article 9(4) was

---

[142] Bayefsky, *Op.Cit.* 1993, 54.
[143] Human Rights Committee, *Maroufida v. Sweden*, Communication No. 58/1979, Views 9 April 1981.
[144] Human Rights Committee, *V.M.R.B. v. Canada*, Communication No. 236/1987, Views 25 June 1987.
[145] Human Rights Committee, *Giry v. Dominican Republic*, Communication No. 193/1985, Views , para. 20.

also violated because Hamel was unable to take proceedings before a court to determine the lawfulness of his arrest.[146] This thinking about detention should have been given effect by the Supreme Court in the *Ahani* case.

Nowak argues that in the Hammel case CCPR article 12.4, right to freedom of movement, could have been applied to protect a long term non-citizen resident – resident for 19 years - from expulsion because the State of residence had become his "home." [147] This thinking was relevant for the Supreme Court considering the case of *Chiarelli*, although the HRC itself would subsequently take a weaker position in *Stewart v. Canada*.

Except for the views in the later *Giry* case, there are echoes of the HRC decisions in General Comment 15/27, "Position of Aliens," which appeared in 1986.

A large number of Western States have put reservations on CCPR article 14, right to fair trial when ratifying the treaty, which has resulted in caution by the HRC in its application.[148] Although the concept of a fair and independent hearing for the adjudication of rights has been applied broadly by the Committee in some situations, it has not been so applied in expulsion or extradition situations. See, for example, article 14 discussed in HRC *V.M.R.B. v. Canada*, above. International treaty bodies are not immune from factoring "political convenience" into their decisions when under political pressure from treaty member States – but that must be another story.

---

[146] Human Rights Committee, *Hammel* v. *Madagascar*, Communication No. 155/1983, Views 3 April 1987 , at para. 19.4, 20.
[147] Nowak, *Op. Cit.*, 1993, 230.
[148] *Ibid*, 237.

Canada had not yet joined the Organization of American States so that the more stringent due process and court access obligations clearly present in the American Declaration of Rights and Duties of Man were not in force. Nonetheless, there were established HRC concerns about the due process contained in CCPR articles 9(4) and 13 as they applied in expulsion situations, including extradition, that continue to arise throughout the subsequent Canadian Supreme Court case law, including the HRC views on *Ahani* v. *Canada* in 2004.

There is no formal report from the examination of Canada by the HRC in 1990. At the time, the Committee provided a Summary Record in which its questions and residual concerns are recorded.[149] There were questions about the legislative arrangements for implementing the obligations of the Covenant. The government gave assurances that:

> "The Canadian Charter of Rights and Freedoms had been significantly influenced by and in many ways reflected the Covenant. The Supreme Court of Canada had itself emphasized that point in its judgments. ... [150]

At the same time, some cautions were now noted:

> "Mr Prado Vallejo had asked whether all the rights enshrined in the Covenant were guaranteed in the Canadian Charter ... and the Canadian Bill of Rights. In fact, those two instruments did not guarantee all the rights enshrined in the Covenant,

---

[149] Official Records of the Human Rights Committee, 199/1991, Volume 1, UN, 1995, 8 – 18.
[150] *Ibid* para. 26.

because the legislative process concerned was a very complicated one ..."[151]

The Human Rights Committee asked about *Charter* s. 1 and its compatibility with the Covenant arrangements for emergencies, and asked questions about the role of the Human Rights Act and its Commission and its role in comparison with the *Charter*. There were concerns about the rights of aboriginal peoples, but no serious concerns about the rights of non-citizens in 1990.

---

[151] *Ibid* para. 81.

4. The Swing from Singh Era

From 1988 to 1992 there was a large turnover in justices. By 1992, the Supreme Court had been transformed by new appointees. Chief Justice, Brian Dickson retired in 1990. Bertha Wilson and Jean Beetz retired in 1988 and 1991 respectively. Between 1987 and 1992, seven new justices were appointed. In July 1990, Justice Lamer   was appointed Chief Justice. Several appointments came after 1989 when changes to the *Immigration Act 1976* took effect.[152] Newcomer Justice Iacobucci brought government experience with immigration matters.[153]   Frank Iacobucci had been the Deputy Minister of Justice when Justice Canada was intimately involved with changes to the *Immigration Act* that took effect in law in early 1989. It is hard to believe that this and other appointments were not a factor in the "Swing from Singh" reported by Eliadis. Yet as previously noted, in the Schmidt decision other Justices were present and other factors were at play in a test for limiting *Charter* rights in extradition.

As noted, major changes to the Immigration Act resulting from the then Bills C-55 and C-84 took effect January 1, 1989 providing a new legal and political context. In addition, large numbers of asylum seekers entered Canada across the border from the US attracting media attention with headlines like "Floods" or "Hordes". There was a series

---

[152] Others appointed were Claire L'Heureux Dube 1987, John Sopinka 1988,Peter Cory 1989, Beverley McLachlin 1989, William Stevenson 1990, Frank Iacobucci 1991, John Major 1992.

[153] Prime Minister Brian Mulroney appointed Frank Iacobucci from the University of Toronto Law School to be Deputy Minister of Justice in 1985. When Deputy Minister of Justice, his department was responsible for preparing major amendments to the *Immigration Act 1976*, and ensuring these complied with the Constitution.

of negative public displays against asylum seekers.[154] This can only have put public pressure on a Supreme Court which itself had implicitly recognized the role of Canadians in its "shocks the conscience of Canadians" test in the *Schmidt* case.

The Supreme Court with new Justices arriving took the trends of *Schmidt* a further step away from international human rights obligations in the 1991 extradition case of *Kindler*. Largely unaware of the import of the extradition cases, refugee advocates were not present and only Amnesty International was intervener. The link from refugees between what Canada does and the consequential violation of rights elsewhere was buried in the earlier judgment of *Singh et al.*

In 1992, with more newly appointed Justices and a climate of public hostility towards refugees, the Supreme Court was challenged to ensure rights for refugees and other non-citizens in the case brought forward by the Council of Churches, *Canadian Council of Churches* v. *M.E.I.* On a personal note, the appointment of Frank Iacobucci to head the court which was to hear the Churches court action, and the media displays of public opposition to refugees so different from the positive public reaction to Indochinese refugees in 1979-1980, felt like an orchestrated plan.

Within months of *CCC* v. *M.E.I.*, the Court was challenged by an individual seeking protection for his non-citizen's CCPR rights as a long term resident facing deportation – the case of *Chiarelli*. But first, we will consider the three extradition cases.

---

[154] David Matas with Ilana Simon, *Closing the Doors: The Failure of Refugee Protection ",* Toronto: Summerhill Press, 1989, 87-160.

Kindler and Extradition 1991

A series of three extradition cases around 1991, Kindler, Ng and Cox, raised questions of the application of the *Charter* to extradition to the United States to face the death penalty. Key among these 1991 cases, *Kindler* established the reasoning of the Supreme Court on extradition.[155] Surprisingly, the Court applied the approach offered by Justice LaForest in the *Schmidt* case for adjudicating the *Charter s.7* rights to life, liberty and security of the person: whether it would breach the principles of fundamental justice to extradite to a country where the person would be treated in a fashion that "shocks the conscience" of Canadians. However, in the Kindler case, the test was applied to a person whose right to life, a fundamental right, was threatened by the death penalty, a penalty almost entirely abolished in Canada, but not abolished in the US.

Key international rights at issue included the CCPR Art.6 right to life with its built in due process right and CCPR Art. 7 no cruel treatment which can also relate to the death penalty, as well as CCPR Art.9 right to liberty and security of the person. The rights to liberty and to no double trial had been at issue in *Schmidt*. The stand-alone American Declaration article I substantive right to life, liberty and security of person was also now at issue as was the article XVIII right to court protection of fundamental rights.

Kindler was found guilty of murder by a court in Pennsylvania and the jury there recommended the death penalty. Before sentencing, Kindler escaped to Canada where he was subsequently arrested. The Canadian extradition judge allowed the U.S.'s application for extradition. The Minister of Justice of Canada, after

---

[155] *Kindler* v. *Canada*, [1991] 2 S.C.R. 779.

reviewing the material supplied by Kindler, ordered his extradition pursuant to s. 25 of the *Extradition Act* without seeking assurances from the U.S. under the extradition treaty between the two countries that the death penalty would not be carried out. The Supreme Court appeal was to determine whether the Minister's decision to proceed without assurances from the U.S. that the death penalty would not be applied, violated Kindler's rights under s.7 or s.12 of the *Charter*. The Supreme Court confirmed the extradition and found that *Extradition Act* s.25 did not infringe s.7 or s.12 of the *Charter*. There was confused thinking on *Charter* s.7 & 12 and division among the Justices.

The majority of justices found that Kindler's *Charter* s.7 life liberty and security of the person was compromised by his expulsion. In contrast with the international rights perspective, the majority ruled that any consequential cruel treatment by the US would not be a violation of Kindler's rights by Canada. For these justices, the issue was whether the impairment of s.7 rights would shock the conscience of Canadians. They found the *Charter* applied to the decision of the Minister to surrender a person to another State, but, perversely, that the right to protection from cruel and unusual treatment or punishment has no application to s.25 of the *Extradition Act* or to the ministerial decisions it permits. They found that extradition by the Minister without assurances that the death penalty will not be applied does not offend the fundamental principles of justice in s.7 of the *Charter*. To justify the decision, these justices noted that Canada must not become a safe haven for criminals. Such statements go only so far as providing a legitimate purpose. A legitimate purpose is only part of the appropriate use of *Charter* s.1 to justify limitation of rights. Also, section 1 was not formally applied. In their words:

"While the *Charter* applies to extradition matters, including the executive decision of the Minister that effects the fugitive's surrender, the guarantee against cruel and unusual punishment found in s. 12 of the *Charter* has no application to s. 25 of the *Extradition Act* or to ministerial acts done pursuant to that section. The decision to surrender a fugitive under s. 25 does not constitute the imposition of cruel and unusual punishment by a Canadian government. The purpose and effect of s. 25 is to permit the fugitive to be extradited to face the consequences of the judicial process elsewhere. The punishment, if any, to which the fugitive is ultimately subject will be punishment imposed, not by the Government of Canada, but by the foreign state."

" ... Since the *Charter*'s reach is confined to the legislative and executive acts of Canadian governments, to apply s. 12 directly to the act of surrender to a foreign country where a particular penalty may be imposed would be to give the section extraterritorial effect."

" ... Section 25 of the Extradition Act, which permits the extradition of fugitives without assurances that the death penalty will not be applied in the requesting states, does not offend the fundamental principles of justice enshrined in s. 7 of the Charter. ... Further, while in some cases it may be mandatory for the Minister to seek death penalty assurances, the variance between cases supports legislation which accords to the Minister a measure of discretion on the question of whether such assurances should be demanded."[156]

---

[156] *Ibid*, 782-783.

There was no discussion of international standards for limits on rights or of the Oakes test. It is not enough to have a legitimate purpose in legislation. The measure must also be necessary, given alternatives that impact less on the right in question. Finally, the measure must be proportionate given the extent of the impairment of the right. In the Kindler case, there is no word on the necessity of the extradition for the stated purpose: "to permit the fugitive to be extradited to face the consequences of the judicial process elsewhere." There is no discussion of the proportionality of extradition when the right to life is threatened by the death penalty, especially when the death penalty is one that Canada had abandoned except for a military offence. Implicitly, Canada had deemed the death penalty to be always disproportionate for any other crime than a military offence.

The new test applied is a long way from the international test and the *Oakes* test under *Charter* s.1. It is an interpretation that moved *Charter* s.7 away from the international rights that should be given effect by this section of the *Charter*. This new formulation with "principles of fundamental justice" in a balancing game governed by uncertain rules is too flexible for the protection of fundamental human rights like life. It seems tantamount to accepting that the public mood of the moment will be a factor in determining the protection of fundamental rights of an individual at risk.

In support of its decision, the Court selectively drew from the UN Model Treaty on Extradition.[157] It noted that the treaty left States the option of obtaining or of not obtaining

---

[157] UN General Assembly, Model Treaty on Extradition, UN Doc. A/RES/45/116, 14 December 1990, Annex.

assurances that the death penalty would not be applied.[158] Ironically, the same model treaty also requires mandatory refusal of extradition if some international human rights are at issue. In particular, the same model treaty requires that a person not be surrendered if there is a real risk of torture or cruel or unusual treatment or punishment or if the person will not enjoy rights in criminal proceedings in accordance with CCPR article 14.[159] The majority of the Court selectively used parts of this evidence and ignored the reference to CCPR rights which spoke directly to protection from torture or cruel treatment and thus spoke directly to *Charter s.12* which was before the court.

In a minority opinion which also fails to give full effect to international rights obligations, Sopinka j. argued that *Charter* s.12 protection from cruel treatment need not be decided because the case is best dealt with under the *Charter* s.7 right to life, liberty and security unless deprived according to the fundamental principles of justice. He could have pointed out the view of the UN HRC that cruel treatment may arise in the application of the death penalty but that in this case situation it did not. He did not go so far. However, he rightly argued that the "shock the conscience" test is problematic:

---

[158] " (d) If the offence for which extradition is requested carries the death penalty under the law of the requesting State, unless that State gives such assurance as the requested State considers sufficient that the death penalty will not be imposed or, if imposed, will not be carried out;" *Ibid,* Art.4., Mandatory grounds for refusal.
[159] "(f) If the person whose extradition is requested has been or would be subjected in the requesting State to torture or cruel, inhuman or degrading treatment or punishment or if that person has not received or would not receive the minimum guarantees in criminal proceedings, as contained in the International Covenant on Civil and Political Rights, article 14;" *Ibid*, Art.3, Mandatory grounds for refusal.

> "Principles of fundamental justice are not limited by
> public opinion of the day."[160]

He argued that *Charter* s.1 will rarely allow extradition to
the death penalty. This approach gives some effect to the
American Declaration right to life and to the CCPR limit on
rights. His is the argument that, with variations, prevailed
ten years later in the *Burns* extradition case. This argument
also appeared subsequently for the rather different
situation of deportation of a refugee at risk of torture in
Suresh.

In another minority opinion, Justice Cory with Justice
Lamer set out extensive arguments for why *Charter* s.12
would be violated. These arguments about protection from
torture come closer to giving effect to the international
right. They use the notion of a link between Canada and
consequences elsewhere that the Court had developed in
Singh et al. Several of the extensive arguments later
reappeared for the majority in the *Burns* case. However, in
the *Burns* case, these arguments were used in favour of
Charter s.7 right to life rather than in favour of s.12 and
protection from cruel treatment. Surprisingly, these
arguments did not reappear in the 2001 case of *Suresh*
when protection from torture was clearly the dominant
right at issue.

The majority justices gave some effect to the international
right to life, CCPR Art. 6, and the international right to
liberty and security of the person, CCPR Art. 9. They did
not apply *Charter* s.7 so as to give best effect to the
international treaty rights when they blended the
substantive international rights and the due process right
in a balancing process. The majority of justices failed to

---

[160] *Kindler, Op.Cit.* 791.

apply the international standard for limiting the rights at issue because they failed to apply the Court's own *Oakes* test to these distinct substantive rights: life; liberty; and, security of the person. The majority failed to interpret the *Charter* so as to give effect to and to ensure the international right to protection from torture or cruel treatment in expulsion, CCPR Art. 7, (as interpreted with the CCPR article 2 obligation to ensure rights), and as established by the Convention against Torture Art. 3.

The Court missed the opportunity to ensure an effective judicial remedy for rights via the distinct due process rights of *Charter* s.7 and the right to a judicial remedy of *Charter* s.24. The judicial remedy required by international human rights obligations would have protected the individual from acts of the authorities that might violate the rights – like the Minister surrendering Kindler to the death penalty. The lack of any reference to *Charter* s. 10 that promises *Habeas Corpus* to anyone in detention may have contributed to the outcome.

On the positive side, one might speculate that the minority justices' reasoning may have helped international treaty body members to develop their own international human rights case law.[161] The outcome for Kindler was largely consistent with the international perspective – as we shall see. But the correct outcome for the person is not good enough. A correct outcome for the individual does not always meet the test of giving effect to and of ensuring the international rights involved for "everyone". The approach which the Court entrenched for extradition established constraints on future related cases. It spilled over into refugee expulsion situations where the same fundamental *Charter* s.7 rights were at issue.

---

[161] See HRC *Ng* v. *Canada, Op.Cit. 1994.*

It is important to pause here and to note some implications for the last chapter where this essay considers whether there are measures which Canada is now required to take in order to meet its obligations to give effect to and to ensure the international rights.

As a layman, I notice that a lawyer is charged with seeking the best outcome for a client. Lawyers for an appellant and a respondent must work within the Court's established pattern and framework. Any novel arguments will be secondary. Thus any new factors and any major change to the approach will tend to come from the positions presented by interveners like Amnesty International or the Canadian Council for Refugees. Yet intervention is itself limited. Even at the time when the Council of Churches intervened in *Singh et al*, the interveners were selected by the Court, limited in number, limited in the size of the submissions they could make, and limited in the time to speak in the proceedings. Interveners will work with one or the other of the parties and they will be reluctant to undermine or contradict the general approach taken by this party. So any opportunity for a change in the court's approach by intervention is limited. Once the direction of case law around *Charter s.7* is set by the court, submissions to the Supreme Court cannot easily change or correct it.

The Supreme Court's comfort with ministerial discretion and restricted judicial review as the means to adjudicate and protect a fundamental Constitutional right ran counter to the international obligation to ensure an effective judicial remedy and to allow court protection for a right threatened by the authorities. The majority of justices noted the lower court review of the Minister's decision, but they did not ensure that the lower court provided an effective judicial remedy for the rights at issue. They could have. There was flexibility in the "standard for review" that the Court went on subsequently to develop in *Pushpanathan*.

The "balancing" within *Charter* s.7 so as not to "shock the conscience of Canadians" was particularly dangerous for non-Canadians. As we shall see, by *Suresh*, the Court had found a way to include some views from international bodies, at arms length from the public hostility. But it did so by considering these views as factors or values in a multi factor balancing operation. It did not give effect to the limits that are an essential part of international rights. The Court did not develop a principled approach about what is "proportionate."

The Council of Churches was hardly aware of this case at the time. The relevance of extradition to its refugee rights cause was not understood. Moreover, the Council was pre occupied in fundraising and preparing for the decision on its own court challenge before the Supreme Court.

The approach of the Supreme Court to *Kindler* can be contrasted with the views of the UN Human Rights Committee when the case arrived before it.[162] The UN case law on this and the two other Canadian extradition cases of the time, those of *Ng* and *Cox*, has been summarized along with the individual views of some members.[163] The cases have also been considered and commented upon in comparison with Canadian law, but not from my international obligation test perspective.[164] Although

---

[162] Human Rights Committee, *Kindler v. Canada*, Communication No. 470/1991, Views 18 November 1993, UN Doc. CCPR/C/48/D/470/1991 (1993).

[163] Manfred Nowak, "The Activities of the UN Human Rights Committee: Developments from 1 August 1992 to 31 July 1995", 16 HRLJ 377, 1998, 385-387.

[164] Joanna Harrington, "How Canadian Lawyers Can Contribute to the

Canada was not found in violation of the CCPR in the case of Kindler, the positions taken by the HRC under the CCPR contrast with the views of the Supreme Court under the *Charter*. Here is the HRC view on CCPR rights and extradition:

> "If a person is lawfully expelled or extradited, the State party concerned will not generally have responsibility under the Covenant for any violations of that person's rights that may later occur ... However, if a State party takes a decision relating to a person within its jurisdiction, and the necessary and foreseeable consequence is that that person's rights under the Covenant will be violated in another jurisdiction, the State party itself may be in violation of the Covenant. That follows from the fact that a State party's duty under article 2 ... would be negated ... ." Para. 6.2

The key point is that the obligation of the State to the CCPR right is spelled out. It is to ensure the CCPR rights for the individual. That is not an obligation spelled out for the Supreme Court with respect to the *Charter*. As we noted in chapter 2, the Supreme Court Act would permit the court to ensure individual rights, but it does not require that. The HRC continues, modelling what it means to give effect to rights in a decision:

> " ... it was not intended that article 13 of the Covenant, which provides specific rights relating to the expulsion of aliens lawfully in the territory of a State party, should detract from normal extradition

---

Effectiveness fo the UN Human Rights Committee", in, *The measure of International Law: Effectiveness, Fairness and Validity*, 2002, 132, 2004, 143-152.

arrangements. None the less, whether an alien is required to leave the territory through expulsion or extradition, the general guarantees of article 13 in principle apply, as do the requirements of the Covenant as a whole." Para. 6.6

In other words, all CCPR rights must be ensured in expulsion or extradition. This is very different from the view taken by the Supreme Court in *Chiarelli*, later. In particular, the HRC notes that the CCPR article 6 right to life and related sub article 6.2 due process are engaged:

" ... If Mr. Kindler had been exposed, through extradition from Canada, to a real risk of a violation of article 6, paragraph 2, in the United States, that would have entailed a violation by Canada of its obligations under article 6, paragraph 1. Among the requirements of article 6, paragraph 2, is that capital punishment be imposed only for the most serious crimes, in circumstances not contrary to the Covenant and other instruments, and that it be carried out pursuant to a final judgment rendered by a competent court." Para. 14.3

Although the HRC was not yet willing to say that CCPR article 7 cruel and unusual treatment will always be at issue when the death penalty is at issue at this point in its case law, it did say that in individual circumstances cruel treatment could arise.

The Supreme Court went on to use the same *Kindler* arguments to allow Canada to extradite *Ng* to the US, but in slightly different circumstances. In the case of *Ng*, the consequence of the extradition was to expose Ng to cruel treatment - a cruel form of the death penalty - in violation of CCPR Art.7.

The HRC decision *Ng v. Canada* has echoes of the dissenting opinions of Sopinka and Cory in the Supreme Court *Kindler* case, but has HRC reasoning which has become more secure and confident since the HRC's *Kindler v. Canada* case:

> "... the Committee observes that what is at issue is ... whether by extraditing Mr. Ng to the United States, Canada exposed him to a real risk of a violation of his rights under the Covenant. States parties to the Covenant will also frequently be parties to bilateral treaty obligations, including those under extradition treaties. A State party to the Covenant must ensure that it carries out all its other legal commitments in a manner consistent with the Covenant. The starting point for consideration of this issue must be the State party's obligation, under article 2, paragraph 1, of the Covenant, namely, to ensure to all individuals within its territory and subject to its jurisdiction the rights recognized in the Covenant." [165]
> "If a State party extradites a person within its jurisdiction in such circumstances that as a result there is a real risk that his or her rights under the Covenant will be violated in another jurisdiction, the State party itself may be in violation of the Covenant." [166]

Here, the HRC established clearly the link between the actions of a deporting or extraditing State and what happens in another country. These HRC views took a stronger position about cruel treatment and the death penalty:

---

[165] *Ng* v. *Canada, Op. Cit.* 1994, para. 14.1.
[166] *Ibid,* para. 14.2.

"... by definition, every execution of a sentence of death may be considered to constitute cruel and inhuman treatment within the meaning of article 7 of the Covenant; on the other hand, article 6, paragraph 2, permits the imposition of capital punishment for the most serious crimes. Nonetheless, the Committee reaffirms ... that, when imposing capital punishment, the execution of the sentence "... must be carried out in such a way as to cause the least possible physical and mental suffering." [167]

Two international rights are at issue, corresponding with *Charter s.7* and *s.12*. It will be always necessary to ensure the *Charter s.12* right to no cruel treatment or punishment which can be at issue for the death penalty.

The UN HRC was silent on the issue of effective judicial remedy. The HRC noted, in deciding whether a remedy in Canadian law was available for admissibility purposes in its *Kindler* decision, that the Canadian government submission stated that at that time it was possible to use *Habeas Corpus*.[168] In a later 2003 deportation context, the HRC found that the lack of access to a court prior to deportation to the death penalty was a violation of the right to an effective judicial remedy by Canada.[169] To my mind the HRC was still not quite clear enough on the obligation I see in the CCPR behind that 2003 decision. "Ensuring" a fundamental right under threat by actions of public officials, like expulsion, requires ensuring effective access to a court which can adjudicate the situation.

---

[167] *Ibid,* para. 16.2.
[168] HRC, *Suresh v. Canada, Op.Cit.*, 1993, para. 8.4
[169] HRC, Judge v. Canada, Op.Cit. 2003.

CCC v. Canada 1992

Canadian Council of Churches v. *M.E.I.* [170] arose from a case launched in 1989. The case was preceded by sweeping legislative changes. There had been massive opposition to these legislative changes.[171] Bill C55 had restructured refugee determination procedures and allowed some asylum seekers to be "weeded out" by the authorities before having a refugee status determination hearing if they failed to meet defined "eligibility" or "admissibility" criteria.[172] For many of us in the NGO world, this "weeding out" seemed contrary to equal treatment in the application of the American Declaration right to seek and receive asylum – a right which, as we have seen, must be in accordance with the laws of the country and international agreements. In the initial legislation, the "weeding" was to be carried out by a mixed hearing involving an immigration official and a tribunal Board member. The Board member would later be dropped in further amendments to the law.[173] Bill C84 allowed the detention of non-citizens arriving in Canada without the designated identity documentation. It provided for mandatory detention of non-citizens certified by two Ministers as posing a criminal or security threat, and required their deportation if a Federal Court judge found the opinion of the Ministers "reasonable". To respond to smuggling of refugees, the legislation gave the government greatly increased powers for search and seizure, much larger jail terms and fines for smugglers and transportation

---

[170] *Canadian Council of Churches* v. *Minister of Employment and Immigration*, January 23, 1992, [1992] 1 S.C.R. 236.

[171] Kelley and Trebilcock, *Op. Cit. 1998*, 418-422.

[172] *Ibid*, 416.

[173] In its later *Deghani* ruling, the changed Court found due process not necessary and the government responded by introducing legislative changes to remove the tribunal member from this hearing.

companies.[174] Efforts by NGOs to have the legislation "give effect" to family rights, children's rights and rights to protection from torture or cruel treatment as rights and to due process in expulsion as of right had been largely disregarded. Access to judicial remedies had been restricted by requiring a lower court judge to identify and to certify an issue before a case could proceed to an appeal court. In other words, a trial judge had to request the appeal of the case before him or her.

I traveled to Ottawa weekly for the Inter-Church Committee for Refugees to monitor the mid week house committee hearings. Later, I traveled across the country to places chosen by the Senate Committee to monitor hearings before it. Almost all testimony before these hearings on Bills C55 and C84 argued that the proposals were unconstitutional in some way. For example, I was present to hear testimony before the Senate Committee by a team of four Constitutional law professors from various Law Schools, including David Beatty. Many expected court challenges. Justice Canada had told parliament that the provisions were Constitutional. Legislators had voiced the expectation that the courts would resolve any problems.

Buoyed on by the body of concerns and with hope in the Court from the *Singh et al* case, the Canadian Council of Churches placed the range of concerns about Charter rights and freedoms before the Federal Court, Trial Division, as a constitutional challenge on January 3, 1989. The case was on behalf of refugees. It was essentially asking that their rights be given effect and ensured. The argument was made that refugees were "inherently vulnerable" and would have difficulty raising the many concerns themselves.[175]

---

174 Kelly and Trebilcock, *Op.Cit. 1998*, 417-18.
175 Canadian Council of Churches, "Application for Leave to Appeal", C.

A condition of the Council of Churches in supporting this court action was that the concerned church groups must raise the necessary funding themselves. With coordination from a joint committee of the Canadian Council of Churches and the then Inter-Church Committee for Refugees, this "court action" used sales of T-shirts, posters and buttons, and fundraising dinner gatherings and auctions in church basements across the country to raise the funds to finance the case. The slogan and the buttons proclaimed "Rights for Refugees". There was a mood within at least a sector of the public in favour of the court action.

The government responded by a bringing a motion before the court to strike out the Statement of Claim because the Council lacked the standing to bring action and because the Statement disclosed no reasonable cause. The government motion was initially defeated before the Trial Division of the Federal Court, but was appealed to the Federal Court of Appeal. The issues there were (1) can the CCC act for refugees (does it have "standing") and (2) is there "reasonable cause for action"? The Federal Court of Appeal found several allegations "speculative" and opined that claimants could raise these issues themselves. It limited the Statement of Claim to four issues. Both parties appealed. The Supreme Court heard the case in 1991.

The Supreme Court judgment, released in 1992 begins:

> "At issue on this appeal is whether the Canadian Council of Churches should be granted status to proceed with an action challenging, almost in its entirety, the validity of the amended Immigration Act, 1976, which came into effect January 1, 1989."

24, page 24.

The key international obligations here are those set out in my international test for a court decision – in particular the CCPR Art. 2 obligation to ensure CCPR rights. This case asked the Court to use the *Charter* to give effect to rights for refugee claimants and to ensure the right to effective judicial protection of their rights.

In its judgment in early 2001, the Supreme Court acknowledged a Constitutional responsibility of the courts, but did not acknowledge a responsibility to ensure the individual's right to a judicial remedy from acts of authority that might violate rights:

> "Parliament and the legislatures are thus required to act within the bounds of the constitution and in accordance with the Canadian Charter of Rights and Freedoms. Courts are the final arbiters as to when that duty has been breached."

The court rejected this opportunity to "respect and ensure" and "give effect" to individual rights as the *Charter* interpreted with the international obligations would require. Focusing on procedural matters, the Court reviewed other States' practices with respect to public interest litigation. It concluded that there must be (1) a serious public issue (2) a genuine interest but (3) no other reasonable and effective way to bring the issue before the Court. The relatively high threshold adopted for the last component of this test evaded the obligation to "ensure" international rights. Despite the Canadian Council of Churches' submissions, the Court accepted the Federal Court of Appeal's optimistic opinion that individual refugee claimants could bring forward issues because they were bringing constitutional issues before the courts daily. The Supreme Court noted:

"the basic purpose of public interest standing is to
ensure that legislation is not immunized from
challenge. Here there is no such immunization as
plaintiff refugee claimants are challenging the
legislation."

We can note that it took 7 years for the Court to begin to
deal with family and children's rights issues in the *Baker*
case and it took the Court 10 years to address protection of
a refugee from torture in expulsion in *Suresh*. Immunizing
from challenge in the short term was the consequence of
the Court's decisions in this and in later cases such as
Chiarelli. Having denied standing, the Court reflected on
the concerns raised:

"A party who did have standing might well find in
this vast broadside of grievances some telling shots
that would from the basis for a cause of action
somewhat wider than that permitted by the Federal
Court of Appeal."

To my mind, the obligation to "ensure" the right to an
effective judicial remedy goes beyond noting that claimants
may raise the existence of a right elsewhere. Also, when
examining other practices, the Court failed to consider the
nature of the international complaints procedure afforded
by the Inter-American Commission on Human Rights. The
nature of this procedure is designed to assist the
Commission in its obligation to ensure rights:

"Any person or group of persons or
nongovernmental entity legally recognized in one or
more of the Member States of the OAS may submit
petitions to the Commission, on their own behalf or
on behalf of third persons, concerning alleged

violations of a human right ..."[176]

Although this is not an obligation or treaty right, it is a pertinent model in the international arena. In contrast, the Supreme Court showed that it was aware that parts of the legislation might violate rights, but the court chose not to give the rights effect and it did not "ensure" that there was an "effective judicial remedy" for potential violations. Rather the Supreme Court conveniently assumed that a remedy was available at the Federal Court.

In its 1998 case of *Vriend v. Alberta*[177], the Supreme Court had to examine once again the test for intervention it had used in *Canadian Council of Churches* in 1992. It was in the context of employment discrimination against homosexuals in Alberta. In *Vriend* the Court felt it would be inappropriate to wait for individuals to raise similar factual situations for health and other areas and the majority read sexual orientation as a ground for discrimination into Alberta's law in the face of evidence that the legislature of Alberta had deliberately excluded it. However, as had been the case in *Canadian Council of Churches,* there was no acknowledgment of the OAS practice of ensuring rights by using a very low threshold for third parties to raise human rights complaints. While I applaud the response to discrimination in *Vriend*, I cannot help noticing that this response to a group which the court acknowledges faces discrimination differs from the response to a group like asylum seekers which Canada and its courts have not recognized as a disadvantaged group facing discrimination. International forums recognize asylum seekers and migrants as groups facing

---

[176] Statute of the Inter-American Commission on Human Rights, article 23, OAS Doc. OEA/Ser.L/V/I.4 re.8, 22 May 2001.
[177] *Vriend v. Alberta*, [1998] 1 S.C.R. 493.

discrimination.[178]

The international human rights case law relating to the general challenging of a law advanced some years later. The Inter-American Commission of Human Rights asked the Inter-American Court of Human Rights for an advisory opinion on the legal effects of a law that manifestly violated the obligations that the State had assumed upon ratifying the American Convention on Human Rights. [179]

In passing on its Opinion, the Inter-American Court of Human Rights referred to the primary State obligation with respect to the Convention - to ensure the rights and freedoms therein. This is essentially the argument made in Chapter 2 above with respect to Canada and human rights obligations. On the specific question, the Court advised:

> "The Commission may recommend to a State the derogation or amendment of a conflicting norm that has come to its attention by any means whatsoever, whether or not that norm has been applied to a concrete case." [180]

The Inter-American Court defined "self executing norms" as provisions that affect individuals from the moment the

---

[178] See for example the Action Plan of the World Conference against Racism, Racial Discrimination, Xenophobia and Related Interance, UN, Durban, 2001. See also, David Weissbrodt, *Final Report on the Rights of Non-Citizens*, U.N. Doc. E/CN.4/Sub.2/2003/23 (2003), para. 2.

[179] Inter American Court of Human Rights, "International Responsibility for the Promulgation and Enforcement of Laws in Violation of the Convention (Arts. 1 and 2 of the American Convention on Human Rights)", Advisory Opinion OC-14/94, December 9, 1994, Inter-Am. Ct. H.R. (Ser. A) No. 14 (1994), para. 32-33.

[180] *Ibid* para. 39.

law enters force. The Court distinguished these from "non-self-executing norms" that empower the authorities to take measures. The non self executing norms do not of themselves constitute a violation of human rights.[181]

I pause here to revisit my layman's view about binding or non-binding. One might say the views of the Inter-American Court are non-binding and that they are therefore merely "opinions". But that misses the point I made in chapter 2. A member of the OAS has committed to a system in which the Inter-American Commission and Court have been given statutes and roles and responsibilities which complement their roles and responsibilities as treaty bodies under the American Convention on Human Rights. It is difficult to imagine a more authoritative statement of Canada's obligations under the binding American Declaration than a relevant Advisory Opinion of the Inter-American Court of Human Rights.

With the hindsight of this "opinion," a Supreme Court concerned to fulfill Canada's international human rights obligations would have identified in the Canadian Council of Churches submission those provisions of the then Immigration Act that qualified as self-executing and would have declared these as violating the corresponding *Canadian Charter* rights and freedoms. Interestingly, the Federal Court of Appeal had, in its own *CCC v. M.E.I.* ruling, taken a position more or less compatible with this international opinion.

The Supreme Court's rationale for its conclusion in *Canadian Council of Churches* was that individuals could raise rights issues themselves. In the more politically convenient context of *Vriend*, the Court found there was

---

[181] *Ibid* para. 41-42.

unnecessary hardship for individuals to wait to be discriminated against when it was clear that the law itself would do this. This position comes close to fulfilling the international test which requires ensuring a CCPR right.

At this point, we cannot conclude that the gap has been closed for non-citizens by the later *Vriend* case. The position taken by the Supreme Court on the only case involving non-citizens, *CCC vs. M.E.I.*, did not meet the international obligation to ensure rights as demonstrated by the Inter-American Court advisory opinion. Later cases will show a continuing reluctance to ensure non-citizens rights.

Eliadis[182] rightly regards *Chiarelli* and the later *Dehghani* as the point where the Court swung away from *Singh*. Yet as I have shown, failure to properly apply the international obligations had allowed earlier precedents in *Schmidt, Andrews* and *Kindler*. In the anti-immigration political context at the time of its *CCC* decision, the Court chose to use procedural issues to avoid ensuring rights. The device of using procedural issues to avoid giving effect to rights continued in *Reza* and beyond.

The practice of the "leave" restriction on access to judicial review before the Federal Court remains analogous to the kind of leave restriction on appeals to the Immigration Appeal Board that the Supreme Court had struck down in 1985 in *Singh*. An almost unique restriction in Canadian law for court access was subsequently legislated. It required, and still requires, the certification of an issue by the Federal Court Trial judge rendering judgment as a precondition for access to the higher Federal Court of Appeal. Yet by its *Reza* decision, the Supreme Court left

---

[182] Eliadis, *Op.Cit. 1995*, 136.

access to the Provincial Courts to protect refugee rights by *Habeas Corpus* ambiguous, thereby favouring the Federal Court route rather than ensuring rights by enabling an alternative route.

Canadian Council of Churches v. *M.E.I.* was significant in another way. It began a new dialogue with an international treaty body. The court action challenge by the Council of Churches which had been denied standing by the Supreme Court was sent by the *CCC* to the Inter-American Commission on Human Rights in summer 1992. At least two individual complaints were sent to the Commission during 1992, and other NGOs submitted more individual complaints. Both complaints from the Council of Churches raised the right to an effective judicial remedy. The case of *Joseph* v. *Canada*, which lost on the issue of admissibility, anticipated the subsequent case of *Baker* before the Supreme Court of Canada. It raised family and children's rights as well as the right to seek and receive asylum.[183] The second case, known to me and described here only as "A", was subsequently settled by the government and the complaint was withdrawn from the Inter-American Commission on condition that there be no publicity.[184] This second case raised an issue relating to the right to seek and receive asylum. New evidence about an asylum seeker's case could not be introduced after the case had been heard. Issues from both these cases were subsequently addressed by the Inter-American Commission in its 2000 Report. As noted

---

[183] IACHR *Joseph* v. *Canada, Op.Cit. 1993*

[184] "A" was a refugee claimant who had compelling new evidence of a fear of persecution after his refugee status hearing. He argued that he had no mechanism whereby this new evidence on refugee status could be taken into account so that "A" had no effective remedy for the rights at issue.

in the introduction, the Council of Churches and the Inter-Church Committee for Refugees remained active in encouraging international jurisprudence. ICCR and the CCC made reports and encouraged other NGOs to make reports to international treaty bodies in preparation for their periodic examinations of Canada. They encouraged others to shape and send refugee and non-citizen cases to international human rights complaints mechanisms. They worked with then Toronto lawyer Sharryn Aiken to assemble a "how to" kit for lawyers about complaining to international treaty bodies. The kit included copies of all the pertinent international case law. This, with action by other NGOs, helped to provide the clarified treaty body positions on non-citizens that emerged after 1992.

Chiarelli 1992

In March 1992, the Supreme Court moved away from *Singh* in deportation situations as well as in extradition by misinterpreting the *Charter* in the *Chiarelli* case.[185] The Court said the *Charter* had no application for a non-citizen's entry or remaining in Canada. The *Immigration Act 1976* was not interpreted so as to give effect to international rights and was left supreme on these matters. This of course was a matter of deportation – not a matter of extradition. Extradition has the legitimate purpose of transferring a person accused of a crime in another country back to that country for a fair trial usually under a treaty providing safeguards. As I will later show, the legitimacy of deportation is presumed rather than demonstrated.

Chiarelli was a long term permanent resident with a record of serious criminal activity. During an appeal of a

---

[185] *Chiarelli* v. *Minister of Employment and Immigration*, March 26, 1992, [1992] 135 N.R. 161.

deportation order, the then Immigration Appeal Board, IAB, referred Constitutional questions about deportation of non-citizens convicted of an offence or issued with a Minister's certificate, to the Federal Court of Appeal.[186] The Federal Court of Appeal found that the Immigration Act provisions on criminals were Constitutional and that the questions about the Minister's certificates could not be raised by the IAB. The Federal Court of Appeal ruled that deportation necessarily implied interference with the liberty of the person. It found that the *Immigration Act* s.83 process, requiring a judge to certify certain questions for any appeal beyond the Federal Court Trial Division, robbed the IAB of its power to allow an appeal on compassionate grounds. Consequently, the person's *Charter* s.7 rights to life, liberty and security of the person had been infringed by a Minister's certificate. The Minister appealed. In its *Chiarelli* decision, the Supreme Court granted the government's appeal.

At the time, the *Immigration Act 1976* gave effect to the international right to effective judicial review. It did so by means of an Immigration Appeal Board, quasi judicial, hearing on the merits followed by judicial review, by leave, on points of law. This hearing had been used by Chiarelli. This appeal before the IAB of the time allowed international rights at risk in expulsion to be adjudicated. They included family rights and protection from risk of torture. This arguably qualified as the simple process required by article XVIII of the American Declaration of Rights and Duties of Man to protect the individual non-citizen from an act by the authorities like expulsion that might violate rights. Indeed, a concern raised by the Canadian Council of Churches in its Court Challenge was

---

[186] The Supreme Court decision includes "1. Legislative Scheme", *Ibid* 164 – 170, and a good account "II Facts and proceedings", *Ibid* 170-178.

that the right given effect by this IAB hearing did not extend beyond permanent resident non citizens to those claiming refugee status. As noted, in the extradition cases prior to Chiarelli's case, the Supreme Court had recognized that *Charter* s.6 and s.7 were at issue in extradition with the possibility of s.12 protection from cruel treatment.

The Supreme Court began with *Charter* s.7 and the requirement that the principles of fundamental justice must be used if there are limits to rights to life, liberty and security of the person.[187] The Court concluded that deportation of non-citizens who have committed serious offences is not to be conceptualized as a deprivation of *Charter* s. 7. This contrasts with the general international interpretation and the view of the Federal Court of Appeal that expulsion invariably impairs a person's rights to liberty and to freedom of movement.[188] It also contrasts with the fact that such deportation invariably requires detention, a deprivation of liberty that reasonably qualifies for *Habeas Corpus* under *Canadian Charter* s.10. The Supreme Court in *Chiarelli* essentially said that for the category of non citizen affected, those convicted of serious crimes, *Charter* s.7 rights cease to exist.

At the same time, the Court also observed that the *Charter* s.12 right to protection from cruel treatment might theoretically arise, but that the right did not arise in *Chiarelli's* particular situation. As we shall see, the Court subsequently failed to give effect to this right when it was

---

[187] "The essence of the respondent's [Chiarelli's] position is that ... [sections of the *Immigration Act*] are contrary to the principles of fundamental justice because they are mandatory and require that deportation be ordered without regard to the circumstances of the offence or the offender." *Ibid* para. 20.

[188] Tom Clark and Sharryn Aiken, *Op.Cit.* 1997, 435.

clearly at issue in the later case of *Suresh*.

As we saw in the UN HRC decisions on *Kindler* and *Ng*, rights do not disappear when a person is accused of a serious offence and they can be at issue in expulsion. If one right is limited, other rights need not be. In 1989 the HRC had made clear in General Comment 15 that almost all CCPR rights are to be enjoyed by non-citizens. In 1996, it would make clear how limits on one right do not affect other rights. It made this latter point in its General Comment about the closely related right to liberty. When liberty is limited, other rights are to be enjoyed to the extent possible.[189] The international right to liberty had been shown at issue in expulsion. To this layman, the right to security of the person is surely impaired, to use the words of Justice Wilson in *Singh*, when a resident is uprooted from a long term place of residence. The Supreme Court interpretation of *Charter* s.7 failed to give effect to the CCPR article 9 and American Declaration article I substantive rights to liberty and security of person at issue.

The Supreme Court also failed to give effect to the international right, CCPR Art.12. , freedom of movement, when dealing with *Charter s.6.* Here, the Court used the significant structural problem in Canadian law which I introduced in chapter 2: the *Charter* s.6 right to freedom of movement is expressly reserved for citizens whereas the corresponding CCPR Art.12(4) is not.

---

[189] Thus, for example, "Persons deprived of their liberty enjoy all the rights set forth in the Covenant [on Civil and Political Rights], subject to the restrictions that are unavoidable in a closed environment." UN Human Rights Committee, General Comment 21 Article 10, UN Doc. HRI/GEN/1/Rev 2, 29 March 1996, para. 3.

In *Chiarelli* the Court noted:

> "The distinction between citizens and non-citizens is recognized in the Charter. While permanent residents are given the right to move to, take up residence in, and pursue the gaining of a livelihood in any province in s. 6(2), only citizens are accorded the right 'to enter, remain in and leave Canada in s. 6(1)."

Most significantly for its future case law, the Court concluded, as if all other rights and freedoms, Canadian or international, had no effect:

> " ... Thus Parliament has the right to adopt an immigration policy and to enact legislation prescribing the conditions under which non-citizens will be permitted to enter and remain in Canada."

It is true, that the *Charter* right applies to citizens. Yet this book has shown that the *Charter* was intended to give effect to the international rights and the international right does not make this distinction. The *Charter* is silent about non-citizens and the *Charter* as a whole was not necessarily at odds with the international obligation. As noted at the end of chapter 1, the early expectation was that protecting the CCPR Art.12 right could require no expulsion of a long term resident because the country had become his or her "home". The Court did nothing to give effect to the international right so interpreted. It might have interpreted *Charter* s.7 security of the person, or the *Immigration Act 1976* so as to give effect to this CCPR obligation as it would subsequently do for some other international rights which became factors or norms in the *Charter s.7* balancing.

Interestingly, parliament had implicitly provided a place for a range of such international rights could be adjudicated. The then existing appeal which a non-citizen could make to the Immigration Appeal Board allowed the matter of length of residence in Canada to be raised as a defense against deportation and so offered in theory an effective remedy for a non-citizens CCPR Art.12(4) right. The government of Canada would point to this hearing in its submissions to international tribunals considering individual complaints from Canada.

The UN Human Rights Committee subsequently found that international rights like family rights and children's rights can be at issue in expulsions such as that of *Chiarelli*. These rights are evidently not limited by *Charter s.6*. However, its interpretation of *Charter s.6* allowed the Supreme Court to put the area of law dealing with deportation of convicted non-citizens out of reach of the supreme law in the manner that Beatty in his book noted some supreme courts do with areas of the law.[190]

There is some subsequent clear and authoritative interpretation of the international right to freedom of movement. In 1996, the UN Human Rights Committee used the substantially similar *Stewart* v. *Canada* case, a case lost by Stewart, as an opportunity to remind Canada and other States about the CCPR Art.12 right to freedom of movement.[191] This individual case law has now been summarized in a General Comment of the HRC interpreting CCPR Art.12 that corresponds with *Charter* s.6:

---

[190] See Beatty, *Op.Cit.*, 85-95.

[191] Human Rights Committee, *Charles E. Stewart* v. *Canada*, Communication No. 538/1993, Views 1 November 1996, UN Doc. CCPR/C/58/D/538/1993.

> "The wording of [Covenant on Civil and Political Rights] article 12, paragraph 4, does not distinguish between nationals and aliens ("no one") [with respect to the right to enter or leave his own country]. Thus, the persons entitled to exercise this right can be identified only by interpreting the meaning of the phrase "his own country". The scope of "his own country" is broader than the concept "country of his nationality". It is not limited to nationality in a formal sense, that is, nationality acquired at birth or by conferral; it embraces, at the very least, an individual who, because of his or her special ties to or claims in relation to a given country, cannot be considered to be a mere alien..."[192]

Surprisingly, given the early expectation about "home" and CCPR article 12(4), in the *Stewart Case* the HRC then went on to find that:

> "But when, as in the present case, the country of immigration facilitates acquiring its nationality, and the immigrant refrains from doing so, either by choice or by committing acts that will disqualify him from acquiring that nationality, the country of immigration does not become "his own country" within the meaning of article 12, paragraph 4, of the Covenant." [193]

---

[192] Human Rights Committee, "General Comment 27, Freedom of movement (Art. 12)", UN Doc. CCPR/C/21/Rev.1/Add.9, (1999), para 20.

[193] HRC, *Stewart v. Canada, Op.Cit.1993,* para. 12.5.

The outcome is surprising because the HRC case reports that Stewart arrived in Canada as a young child of 7 years. It is not that he failed to take advantage of the opportunity to apply for citizenship. His parents failed to give him that status. The HRC case document reports his testimony that he was unaware that he was not a Canadian until immigration officials told him when he had committed a crime. By this time, the criminal act was a bar in Canadian law preventing him from acquiring citizenship.

Whether one regards the outcome in the HRC case right or wrong, clearly the CCPR right to freedom of movement was at issue in Stewart's expulsion and the right was given effect by the HRC in its views. The *Charter* cannot easily be interpreted so as to give effect to this international right and so the *Charter* cannot be used to strike out offending provisions of the *Immigration Act* as had been done in *Singh et al.* To my mind, the best means of ensuring the international right for everyone as intended and in a manner equal to that of all other international rights is by correcting the omission in the *Charter* right. As *Chariell i* shows, having this international right can be extremely important for some non-citizens in Canada.

The facts of Chiarelli's case had raised the concerns subsequently raised by the HRC, above, about persons who cannot be considered a mere alien. He was a long-term permanent resident who would be separated from family members living in Canada, from work-related and other long term friendships developed by residence through his formative adolescent years. At the time of *Chiarelli*, European Court of Human Rights case law had shown that protection from disproportionate impairment of family rights could preclude the deportation of even the most serious criminals after they had served their sentences.[194] True, that was under the European Convention on Rights and Freedoms. In earlier chapters I have supported those who point out that a principled use of international law must avoid picking and choosing convenient case law from favoured treaties. Treaties which Canada has ratified are binding and must have more significant effect. At the same time, it would have been reasonable for the Court to assume, as I did, that it would be only a matter of time before UN and OAS human rights systems adopted a somewhat similar position around expulsion and its effect on similar family rights. Both did.

At the time, an international perspective would have assessed whether the limitation of each right effected was for legitimate purpose, necessary and proportionate – essentially the *Oakes* test in Canadian law. The European Court perspective could have helped the Supreme Court define what is proportionate. The outcome should depend on the circumstances of each case and the rights at issue.

I found it valuable to reflect on the distinction between deportation and extradition. The distinction is rooted in the test for limitation of rights from chapter 2: a limit must be in law, for a legitimate purpose, necessary and proportionate. Extradition of a person accused of a crime to another State where the crime was committed for trial will in most cases be a legitimate purpose. This is what the Supreme Court found in *Kindler*. Beyond this legitimate purpose, there can be questions of necessity, if the trial could take place in Canada or in a third country. Finally, there can be questions around proportionality. However, deportation is different from extradition and the legitimacy

---

[194] *Moustaquim* v. *Belgium*, European Court of human Rights, Series A.152, 30 March 1989.

of the government purpose can appear less compelling.

One has to wonder what legitimate purpose is accomplished by sending back home a resident of Canada who came as a child, became criminalized in Canada as a youth and who served the sentence for the crimes committed in Canada?[195] Why is this person some other country's problem? By its immigration programs, Canada selects some of another country's brightest and best as immigrants to advance its economic and demographic goals. It doesn't seem reasonable to return to a country, whose educated people were taken, one of the offspring of those people who has been raised from a small child in Canada. Such a person has lived a huge fraction of his life in Canada and has been socialized by Canada during adolescence into crime.

It is true that in international law a State may determine who enters State territory and so the State has implicitly a general authority to deport non-citizens. But this does not seem to necessarily authorize the situation that I have just described. Under the pre-UN Charter international law, aliens were the property of their native country. However, the Universal Declaration of Human Rights and the subsequent human rights treaties appear to be an attempt to break with that old approach to "aliens." They establish a new approach and new responsibilities. Now the treatment of everyone – including non-citizens – falls under a State's jurisdiction. The host state is responsible for the rights and freedoms of everyone on its territory. However, the new order is unclear what happens when a host State wishes to forcibly return a non-citizen to a home country. Presumably, the older international law remains. The

---

[195] This is an outline of the case facts in Human Rights Committee *Stewart v. Canada.*

internationally agreed purpose of a criminal justice system is to rehabilitate. If so, is there any obligation on Canada to pay residual rehabilitation costs and the reintegration costs for a criminal returned who has not been fully rehabilitated after serving the sentence? The literature is silent on these issues.

Moreover, extradition is usually by formal treaty agreement. Deportation seldom is. Deportation is usually a one-sided undertaking made by one of the States involved. There will always be some consequential impairment of treaty human rights of the individual deported. Whatever the underlying international law and costs, human rights law is clear. Restriction of rights requires a legitimate purpose. The legitimate purpose for deportation must be stated. For restricting international rights, it will need to be a legitimate international purpose. It will likely be a weaker purpose than the purpose behind an extradition agreement between two States. Yet here again, the literature simply assumes deportation is legitimate.

It follows from such reflection that the conscience of the Canadian public, used by the Supreme Court in the *Chiarelli* case, is not the only factor at play when the individual is of legitimate concern to more than one country. Canadians may find it a reasonable limitation on rights and due process to deport a non citizen who commits a serious crime back to the home country without a formal quasi judicial hearing. Yet an international perspective may set the level of "proportionate" in another place. To get a better sense of "proportionate" we should take a look at the ongoing pattern of deportations of criminalized non-citizens to the Caribbean.

In the 1990s, both Canada and the United States were deporting criminal young men, raised in Canada and the

US, back to their Caribbean countries of origin. A case in point in Canada was one of the accused in the widely publicized "just desserts" shooting which I discussed earlier.[196] The Canadian public was incensed by the reports of the "just desserts" shooting which involving a non-citizen born in a Caribbean country and previously convicted of a serious crime. Caribbean countries had a different perspective on the appropriateness of the sending back of young people who had become criminalized during their adolescence in Canada and the US. The Jamaican ambassador to the US spoke on behalf of Caribbean countries members of CARICOM giving their collective view of similar deportations by the US:

"One area of deep concern for CARICOM states is the problem of deportation. This ... has had a serious impact on the social fabric of many CARICOM countries that lack the resources to deal with the impact of criminal returnees many of which have little ties to the communities to which they are returned. The incidents of deportation from the US to Caribbean countries has increased despite the pleas from Caribbean governments for the US to be sensitive to the capacity of Caribbean law enforcement agencies to deal with the influx of highly experienced "deportees" with access to sophisticated weapons through their existing criminal ties to the US."[197]

---

[196] Kelley and Trebilcock, *Op. Cit.* 1998, 433.
[197] Statement of Dr. Richard L. Bernal, Jamaica's Ambassador To The United States, Embassy of Jamaica, Washington, D.C., before the Subcommittee on the Western Hemisphere House Committee on International Relations May 17, 2000, on the topic of the US and the Caribbean in the New Millennium. Downloaded on October 25,2005, http://www.rism.org/isg/dlp/ganja/resources/AmbassadorWashington.html.

This Jamaican perspective has continued for some years:

> "Increases in the levels of deportation of Caribbean-born immigrants illegally in the United States is having a direct impact on violence in Jamaica according to JA police officials. The island repatriated more than 4,200 Jamaicans in 2004 deported after completing prison sentences in the United States, Canada and the United Kingdom. Assistant Commissioner of Police George Williams pointed to last month's deportation of 40 convicted criminals via charter flight from Louisiana to Jamaica as troublesome. A reported 1,206 persons have been returned to the Jamaican island in 2005." [198]

In this politicized context, Canadian values cannot be perceived as a fair tool for the courts to use. International rights and the corresponding international case law can play an important role in providing an objective basis for a decision involving non-citizens. In this context, the correct decision in extradition or deportation or incarceration of non-citizens must reflect the relevant international jurisprudence.

In the *Chiarelli* decision the court ruled that measures for expelling anyone qualifying for this class of persons, that is, serious criminals, will be Constitutional. In so ruling, the Court authorized the "weeding out" of a group as then Minister Flora MacDonald had promised in 1985 immediately after the decision on *Singh et al.* Although such persons are described as serious criminals, the charges and sentences can be quite varied. Also, they will

---

[198] Jamaica Newsweekly for the week ending June 24th, 2005.

have all served their sentences by the time they can be deported. The Court simply endorsed the government's right and duty to keep out and to expel unwanted aliens. The Court found no circumstances to warrant otherwise:

> "...personal circumstances may vary ... however ... they are ... all persons who fall within the class of permanent residents described in s. 27(1)(d)(ii). They have all deliberately violated an essential condition under which they were permitted to remain in Canada. In such a situation, there is no breach of fundamental justice in giving practical effect to the termination of their right to remain in Canada."[199]

Human rights are not conditional on duties or conditions or presumed contracts. As we shall see reported by Aiken and Scott, the Canadian Council of Churches tried to repair the Court's approach in *Chiarelli* in its later submissions to the Court in the *Baker* case, suggesting that the "immigration context" notion introduced by the Court should be confined to how rights can be limited by *Charter* s.1 rather than as arguments that denied the existence of these rights.[200]

Despite its observation that *Charter* s.12 cruel treatment, might theoretically arise so that torture might be at issue in other cases, the Court went out of its way to point out that the appeal to the IAB which Chiarelli had enjoyed and which might have ensured protection form torture, was not required by the Constitution for anyone in this class.

---

[199] *Chiarelli, Op.Cit. 1992,* para. 26.
[200] Sharryn Aiken and Sheena Scott, "Baker v. Canada (Minister of Citizenship and Immigration) and the Rights of Children," 15. J. Law and Social Policy 211, 2000, 224.

"Although it has been added as a statutory ground of appeal, the executive has always retained the power to prevent an appeal from being allowed on that ground in cases involving serious security interests."

Here, the Supreme Court drew attention to a provision that had given effect to international rights, but then concluded that it was not required under the *Charter*. As pointed out in chapter 2, a Supreme Court is an autonomous part of the State sharing the obligation to give effect to and to ensure international rights and an effective remedy. There was an obligation on Canada to ensure this IAB appeal so as to give effect to the international right. By this decision, the Court paved the way for removal of a hearing that had given some effect to international family rights of this group of non-citizens.

As noted above, the CCPR Art.12.4 right to leave and return should inform the *Immigration Act 1976* so as to protect some non-citizens such as stateless people from deportation. Their rights should be protected. In theory, after the Court's *Baker* decision, to be discussed later, this international right could be treated as a factor to be considered. The international best interest of the child principle was to be considered in the discretionary process at issue in *Baker* allowing persons to remain in Canada on humanitarian and compassionate grounds. However, the CCPR Art. 13 right of all non-citizens requires some level of due process and the American Declaration requires access to a court to adjudicate a right. As the HRC put it:

"In no case may a person be arbitrarily deprived of the right to enter his or her own country. The reference to the concept of arbitrariness in this context is intended to emphasize that it applies to all State action, legislative, administrative and judicial; it guarantees that even interference provided for by law should be in accordance with the provisions, aims and objectives of the Covenant [on Civil and Political Rights] and should be, in any event, reasonable in the particular circumstances..."[201]

In its *Stewart* v. *Canada* ruling in 1996, the HRC did not find a violation of Stewart's family rights (CCPR art. 17 & 23) precisely because it noted that Canada had examined the matter in a hearing before the IAB.[202]

"The deportation of Mr. Stewart will undoubtedly interfere with his family relations in Canada. The question is, however, whether the said interference can be considered either unlawful or arbitrary. ... In its reasoned decision the Immigration Appeal Division considered the evidence presented but it came to the conclusion that Mr. Stewart's family connections in Canada did not justify revoking the deportation order. The Committee is of the opinion that the interference with Mr. Stewart's family relations that will be the inevitable outcome of his deportation cannot be regarded as either unlawful or arbitrary when the deportation order was made under law in furtherance of a legitimate state interest and due consideration was given in the deportation proceedings to the deportee's family connections."

---

[201] HRC, General Comment 27, *Op.Cit. 1999*, para 21.
[202] Human Rights Committee, *Stewart v. Canada*, Communication No. 538/1993, Views 16 December 1996, UN Doc. CCPR/C/58/D/538/1993 (1996), para. 12.10

The IAB hearing allowing family and other rights to be adjudicated prior to *Stewart's* deportation is the very hearing that the Supreme Court said was not required by the Constitution in *Chiarelli*. A year later, in 1997, in the somewhat similar *Canepa* 1997 case before the Human Rights Committee, Canepa alleged the violation of his right to family life.[203] The Committee repeated its observation that there had been due process [the IAB hearing] in Canada:

> "The Committee has noted the State party's argument that the decision to remove the author from Canada was not taken arbitrarily as the author had a full hearing with procedural safeguards and his rights were weighed against the interests of society." [204]

But this time the Committee went further on the fact that CCPR article 17 rights can be at issue:

> "The separation of a person from his family by means of his expulsion could be regarded as an arbitrary interference with the family and as a violation of [CCPR] article 17 if in the circumstances of the case the separation of the author from his family and its effects on him were disproportionate to the objectives of removal." [205]

However, the Committee then examined the facts of this case:

---

[203] Human Rights Committee, *Canepa v. Canada*, Communication No. 558/1993, Views 20 June 1997, UN Doc. CCPR/C/59/D/558/1993, 20 June 1997.
[204] *Ibid,* para. 11.4.
[205] *Ibid,* para. 11.4.

"The author, who has neither spouse nor children in Canada, has extended family in Italy. He has not shown how his deportation to Italy would irreparably sever his ties with his remaining family in Canada. His family were able to provide little help or guidance to him in overcoming his criminal tendencies and his drug-addiction. He has not shown that the support and encouragement of his family is likely to be helpful to him in the future in this regard, or that his separation from his family is likely to lead to a deterioration in his situation. There is no financial dependence involved in his family ties. There appear to be no circumstances particular to the author or to his family which would lead the Committee to conclude that his removal from Canada was an arbitrary interference with his family, nor with his privacy or home."[206]

While the Committee has set out the principles well here, giving effect to these rights, this thinking came too late to help Stewart by ensuring his rights. Stewart did have a separated wife, two children, an ailing mother and a retarded brother in Canada. He was trying to support them while rehabilitating himself from drug abuse. Had the HRC's *Canepa* analysis been applied to the facts of the earlier *Stewart Case*, the HRC would likely have found a violation of Stewart's article 17 right.

There are two points here. First, CCPR article 12 mobility rights and article 17 family rights can be at issue in expulsions. Secondly, the IAB was the place where these rights could be heard. In both *Suresh* and *Canepa*, the Canadian authorities told the HRC that a hearing of these

---

[206] *Ibid,* para. 11.5.

rights had taken place before the then IAB, a quasi judicial tribunal.

The *Chiarelli* judgment allowed government Ministers to trump international rights and *Charter* rights. Ministers could use certificates to designate persons criminals or security risk under the *Immigration Act 1976* s.40.1(1). This labelled the person as falling within a class of non-citizens on the basis of very little evidence. The authorities had only to shown that it was reasonable to suppose that the person qualified as a security risk. If the Federal Court determined that the issuing of the certificate was based on reasonable grounds, s. 40.1(3) and s.40.1(4), the law mandated detention and deportation. The very limited ability to know the case against one and to respond to it, and the restricted judicial review of the issuing of such a certificate were all accepted by the Supreme Court as Constitutional.

This Court decision on Chiarelli's case paved the way for the government to change the legislation to take away the "appeal" to the IAB that the Court had said was not needed by the *Charter*. That government move was aided by public furor arising from media exposure of the story of a non-citizen who allegedly shot a woman in a "Just Desserts" café in Toronto.[207] The non-citizen involved was subsequently acquitted of the charges. The acquittal should have removed the need for a measure to deny such non-citizens an effective judicial remedy. Nonetheless, parliament legislated the appeal hearing out of the *Immigration Act* for this class of persons.

If there were ambiguities in the international standards applicable to the certificate process, the Inter-American

---

[207] Kelley and Trebilcock, *Op. Cit.* 1998, 433.

Commission's 2000 Report clarified the situation for the security certificates. After considering Canada's comments and the Canadian government's reference to the European Court case of *Chahal v. UK* and the Federal Court of Canada case *Jaballah*, the IACHR concluded:

> " ... it is a fundamental principle of due process that the parties engaged in the judicial determination of rights and duties must enjoy equality of arms. A person named in a certificate who is the subject of secret evidence will not enjoy a full opportunity to be heard with minimum guarantees, the essence of the right to due process..."[208]

Despite authoritative international advice in the meantime, including an on site visit by the Inter-American Commission in 1997, a report from the UN Human Rights Committee in 1999 and finally the report from the Inter-American Commission on Human Rights in 2000, the Court moved only a short distance from its *Chiarelli* positions in its 2002 twinned decisions on *Suresh* and *Ahani*. It is true that in the HRC *Ahani* case, the UN Human Rights Committee was able to accept that Security Certificate review process of the Federal Court.[209] However, the security certificate process was, in Ahani's case, a violation of the CCPR Art.9.4 right to have the lawfulness of detention determined without delay.

Reza 1994

The *Reza* case of the Supreme Court came in 1994.[210] It gave the Court a chance to meet the international

---

[208] Inter-American Commission 2000 Report, *Op.Cit.*, para. 156, 157.
[209] HRC, *Ahani v. Canada, Op. Cit.*, para. 10.5.
[210] *Reza v. Canada*, [1994] 2 S.C.R. 394.

obligation to ensure an effective judicial remedy and the obligation to ensure a court determine the lawfulness of detention without delay. The *Canadian Charter* right to *Habeas Corpus* seems unambiguous and blunt in *Charter* s.10, but the Supreme Court managed to deem the different process legislated specifically for non-citizens to be equivalent. Reza can best be understood alongside the lower court *Pieroo* case.

Almost immediately after changes to the Immigration Act came into force in January 1989, *Pieroo,* applied for *Habeas Corpus* to prevent return to Iran where she feared persecution. *Peiroo* was an Iranian woman asylum seeker.[211] She had been found to have no credible basis for a refugee claim, and the adjudicator had issued an exclusion order requiring her to leave Canada. Peiroo argued that the judicial review procedure prescribed in the law did not offer the same protections as the *Habeas Corpus* remedy that should always be available. The Ontario Court (General Division) found no reasonable and probable grounds for complaint by *Pieroo*. The Ontario Court of Appeal found that *Habeas Corpus* was an extraordinary remedy that does not lie when there is an adequate alternative remedy. The *Immigration Act* offered a comprehensive scheme for review and appeal at each stage. This interpretation of Canadian law does not seem compatible with the fact that there is, in the supreme law, *Charter* s.10, a right to *Habeas Corpus* for everyone. The Ontario Court ruling was not compatible with the international obligation of giving effect to and ensuring the right to a simple court procedure that will protect an individual from acts of the authorities that violate fundamental rights.

---

[211] *Pieroo* v. *Canada*, May 29, 1989, 69 O.R. (2d) 253

The *Reza* case allowed the international obligation, blocked at the Ontario Court of Appeal in *Pieroo*, to go before the Supreme Court.

The importance of an impartial testing of the lawfulness of detention has a long history. It includes medieval experiences of despotic monarchs who hid people in secret jails and tortured them on grounds of suspected treason. It includes the behaviour of twentieth century Latin American dictators like Pinochet and the behaviour of a military junta like that in Argentina where individuals disappeared and were tortured presumably in the name of preserving State security. As noted above, the remedy appears in CCPR Art. 9.4:

> "Anyone who is deprived of his liberty by arrest or detention shall be entitled to take proceedings before a court, in order that that court may decide without delay on the lawfulness of his detention and order his release if the detention is not lawful."

As noted above, there is a comparable provision in the *Charter s.10* which reads:

> "Everyone has the right on arrest or detention ... c) to have the validity of the detention determined by way of *habeas corpus* and to be released if the detention is not lawful."

Similarly, as we have seen, *Charter s.24.1* offers a rather weak right to apply to a court:

> "Anyone may apply to a court if any of their *Charter* rights are infringed or denied."

A question arises as to whether refugees and other non-citizens may benefit from these *Charter* provisions in equality with citizens despite the provisions in the *Immigration Act* that are arguably more onerous to use on account of the need to apply for leave or permission to appear before the Federal Court.

The Inter-American Court of Human Rights has taken a firm view of the importance of the right of H*abeas Corpus* in its Advisory Opinion OC-8/87 presumably on account of the Latin American experiences. This interprets for the Americas such binding obligations as American Declaration Art. XXV, which promises a right to have the legality of detention determined by a court and Art.XVIII which promises every person the right to resort to the courts to ensure respect for his legal rights ... and ... a simple brief procedure whereby the courts will protect him from acts of authority that ... violate any fundamental constitutional rights.

The Reza case offered the Supreme Court an opportunity to give effect to and to ensure *Habeas Corpus* for non-citizens. It also offered the Court the chance to give effect to the more general American Declaration Art XVIII right to access a court for protection of fundamental rights from acts of the authorities because Reza had also claimed that fundamental *Charter* rights were violated by the procedures. Both the risks of deportation to torture and incarceration prior to deportation, were at issue. *Charter* s.10 seemed a right to be claimed and the Ontario Courts were clearly a place for *Habeas Corpus* relief. Equally, the Ontario courts were clearly a court that could offer *Habeas Corpus* as the simple effective court remedy promised for rights threatened by the American Declaration of Rights and Duties of Man. Canadian law had the potential to satisfy international obligations until the ruling on the Reza case where the Supreme Court pulled back from that possibility.

Reza had used the legislated procedure in the *Immigration Act 1976* to seek judicial review of a negative administrative decision to prevent deportation to a plausible risk of torture. This administrative procedure was subsequently found wanting in the Baker case. Reza then turned to the Ontario Court. The Ontario Court of Appeal did not name, but gave some effect to the international rights in its judgment. In overturning the decision of the Ontario Court of Appeal, the Supreme Court failed to address the international rights at issue, failed to give them effect and failed to ensure them. It also denied non-citizens the *Charter* right to *Habeas Corpus*.

Reza came from Iran in 1987. At that time, almost all such persons fleeing Iran had a plausible fear of persecution if returned. Yet Reza was somehow found to have no credible basis for claiming refugee status and a deportation order was issued. He applied to the Federal Court of Appeal for leave to set aside the deportation. The Court dismissed his request. He applied to remain on discretionary humanitarian and compassionate grounds, administered by immigration officials, but was turned down. The Federal Court Trial Division refused leave for judicial review of the administrative decision denying Reza's remaining on humanitarian grounds.

Given the widely accepted risks of persecution if such a person was returned to Iran at the time, fundamental rights were plausibly at risk. The right to liberty was accepted as at issue on account of detention in Canada, but there were also risks to the rights to life, liberty and security of the person and the right to no torture or cruel treatment consequential to return, but this court failed to give effect to any of these international rights. It failed to adjust any court access rights so as to ensure the right to a simple court procedure to protect Reza from administrative decision-making that might, as a consequence, put those rights at risk, as American Declaration article XVIII requires.

Reza turned to the Ontario Courts to challenge the constitutionality of the credible basis hearing, source of the decision that allowed the deportation, and of the leave requirement for an appeal to the Federal Court Trial Division. He argued that the legislated process violated *Charter* s.7, 15 and 24.1. The Ontario Court (General Division) allowed a government motion to dismiss the Constitutional challenge of the legislated process. The issue was whether the Court may decline to exercise its jurisdiction and if so, whether to do that in this case. From the international perspective, this is an issue of ensuring the individual's rights. The judgment went on:

> "In the absence of any showing that the available review process and appeal process is inappropriate or less advantageous than the *habeas corpus* jurisdiction of this Court, this Court should, in the exercise of its discretion, decline to grant relief on a *habeas corpus* application. Both jurisprudence and logic would support that this Court should leave the review of immigration matters with the Federal Court of Canada."[212]

The judgment reached the same conclusion with respect to the fundamental *Charter s.7 and s.15* rights that Reza claimed were being violated by the procedure in the *Immigration Act.*

---

[212] *Reza, Op.Cit. 1994*, p. 399.

Reza appealed to the Ontario Court of Appeal where the majority of two judges of the panel of three judges, including Justice Arbour, who is now UN High Commissioner for Human Rights, ruled:

> "there is no principle which justifies a provincial superior court declining jurisdiction simply because the identical remedy could be pursued in the Federal Court, when a constitutional remedy is sought ... before a court fully competent to grant it."[213]

Judge Arbour noted the plausible difficulty in seeking leave for court review as compared with the Ontario Court procedures. This gave some effect to the international rights set out above. It is not mentioned in the decision, but the consequence would have been a large number of non-citizens applying to the Ontario courts for relief by exercising their right to *Habeas Corpus*. Implicit in the Arbour ruling is the notion that a fundamental right to *Habeas Corpus* trumps administrative convenience and some court costs. The dissenting 3rd justice, Justice Abella, who was subsequently appointed to the Supreme Court in 2004, argued that the *Charter* rights could have been raised previously before the Federal Court. Referring to the *Pieroo* case, she said that a judge of the Ontario Court has discretion to hear a case or not hear a case. The Federal Court is the court provided for in the *Immigration Act*.

From an international perspective, *Charter* s. 24 should be applied so as to ensure the international right to an effective remedy for the right to liberty and for fundamental rights. The *Charter* is clear that an individual may go

---

[213] *Ibid,* p. 402.

before any court for relief and may claim *Habeas Corpus* in particular. Limits would require a *Charter* s.1 argument. If the courts both had jurisdiction, the matter was one of choice for the applicant. The majority correctly applied the *Charter* in accordance with international obligations. Abella's analysis moved the law away from international obligations. A court cannot "ensure" an effective judicial remedy for the rights of an individual before it by supposing that another court might have been asked to hear the case. Also, the right to *Habeas Corpus* in the ordinary meaning of the words of the *Bill of Rights* and the *Charter* can mean only *Habeas Corpus*, and *Habeas Corpus* as of right for everyone in equality. It is a sad undermining of a fundamental right to declare it limited for some by the discretion of a lower Court judge.

The Supreme Court generally agreed with dissenting Justice Abella's reasoning.[214] At the same time, in distinction from Abella, the Supreme Court pointed out that the Constitutionality of the requirement to obtain leave before one could have judicial review of one's case by the Federal Court could not be viewed as dealt with by Federal Court proceedings. The Supreme Court failed the obligation to give effect to and to ensure non-citizens rights – here, the rights to *Habeas Corpus* and to an effective judicial remedy. It did so by ignoring that very issue which was before it. In contrast with the Ontario Court of Appeal majority ruling, that reported in its very ruling the inadequacies of the leave process as compared with access to *Habeas Corpus* as of right, the Supreme Court simply side stepped. Similarly, there is no mention of the automatic "stay" of deportation or other action when a case is before the Ontario Court. This was in contrast with the absence of any legislated stay when a case was before the

---

[214] *Ibid*, p. 405.

Federal Court. The majority decision of the Ontario Court of Appeal had noted this, but the Supreme Court failed to notice.

In its 2000 Report, the Inter-American Commission on Human Rights specifically identified the leave requirement for access to the Federal Court for rejected asylum seekers as problematic for international human rights obligations.[215]

It is possible to argue that subsequent adjustment of the nature of judicial review gave some further effect to the international right to an effective court remedy. However, here in its *Reza* decision the Supreme Court ruled that the basis for reviewing the discretion of a lower court judge was whether the judge had given sufficient weight to all relevant considerations. Without further qualification, this is not very helpful. In theory, equal treatment could be a possible basis for seeking a review. However, the *Andrews* ruling can be read as undermining the *Charter* s.15 right to equal treatment before the law. Without equal treatment there can be no predictability of outcome. Thus, when seeking *Habeas Corpus* as a remedy for deportation, there is no guarantee that two similarly situated persons would be treated equally.

---

[215] " ... a number of sources, including several State functionaries as well as practitioners and others working within the system, characterized the leave requirement as providing a form of docket control. A highly reliable source indicated that ...it [Federal Court] tends ot grant leave in 'only the most meritorious' cases." and "... The right of access is a necessary aspect of the right to 'resort to the courts' ... requires available and effective recourse for the violation of a right protected under the [American] Declaration or the Constitution ..." IACHR Report 2000, *Op. Cit.* para. 94 and para. 95.

The outcome in the Supreme Court *Reza* judgment is politically convenient. It does not upset federal versus provincial court roles and the costs incurred by these. It leaves administrative discretion and lower court discretion intact. It preserves a central role for the *Immigration Act* in prescribing the treatment of non-citizens outside the normal operating of the law for citizens. For the individual non-citizen, the decision fails to ensure any one effective court access to protect from acts of the authorities that might violate fundamental rights to life, to no torture by deportation and to freedom.

This tendency of the Supreme Court to avoid and to fail to " give effect" to rights continued in the case of *Baker*.

Summary of International Advice 93 - 99

In this chapter 4 there has been continual reference to international human rights jurisprudence. There can be little doubt that there is a form of dialogue between the Supreme Court and the international treaty bodies. However, the exchanges have a character of pushing or testing the other. As before, this section will establish the timelines between Canadian and international case law.

The landmark judgment by the European Court of Human Rights on extradition to cruel forms of the death penalty was in 1989. It involved the decision of the UK to extradite Soering to the United States where he would have faced treatment while being held on death row which in his case was considered cruel and inhuman. *Soering* v. *UK*, appeared in 1989 before the *Kindler* case. The CCPR treaty text went further than the European treaty text by requiring a State to ensure the rights. Thus the case for non-extradition when rights to life and to no cruel treatment were at issue was stronger under the CCPR than under the

European Convention. The HRC views in *Kindler* v. *Canada* and *Ng* v. *Canada* came later. As could have been predicted, the HRC cases make it clear that the rights to life and to no torture or cruel treatment are at issue in extradition to the death penalty.

International jurisprudence relating to *CCC* v. *M.E.I.* developed after the Supreme Court decision. The Inter-American Court advisory opinion about laws that violate the [American] Convention appeared in 1994. It reinforced obligations in the American Convention which parallel the CCPR with a concept of ensuring rights.

Prior to the Supreme Court's decision on *Chiarelli*, case law of the European Court of Human Rights precluded expulsion of long term residents with records of serious crimes if the consequence would break up an existing unit of close family members. International family and children's rights could be at issue. At the time, the expectation was that CCPR Art. 12(4), right to freedom of movement, would preclude the expulsion of a long term resident non-citizen – at least absent a serious criminal record. The HRC issued its ruling in its *Stewart* v. *Canada* case in 1996 some time after *Chiarelli* case.

In 1993 the Committee against Torture examined Canada after the Supreme Court decision on Kindler and on Chiarelli. Although pertinent questions were raised by the Committee, there were no answers, presumably because decisions were pending at the HRC. The Summary Record of the examination simply says:

> "In connection with article 3 of the Convention [against Torture], members of the Committee requested further information on the action taken by the Government of Canada to ensure

compatibility with the provisions of that article, especially on the issue of non-refoulement. In this connection they recalled that persons who were refused entry or refugee status should not be returned to countries where there was a risk that they might be subjected to torture. Moreover, it was asked whether the Government of Canada considered that extraditing a person to a country where he could face the death penalty subjected that person to inhuman and degrading treatment."
"With regard to article 3 of the Convention, the representative told the Committee that Canada's refugee determination system fully complied with the Convention's requirements relating to torture allegations. ... With regard to the concern raised that a person might be extradited to face the death penalty the representative referred to various debates on the issue in the Human Rights Committee and in the Supreme Court of Canada."[216]

In 1994, only a year later, the Committee against Torture found in *Khan* v. *Canada* that if Canada were to expel Khan, who had not been recognized as a refugee, to Pakistan, it would violate article 3 of the CAT.[217] This obliquely indicated that the Canadian procedures had not been adequate to "ensure" the right to protection from torture by expulsion.

In 1995 the Committee on the Rights of the Child examined Canada and concluded:

---

[216] Concluding observations of the Committee against Torture : Canada, UN Doc. A/48/44, 26/06/93, paras.284-310, para. 293, 301.
[217] CAT, *Khan* v. *Canada*, Communication No. 51/1994, Views 18 November 1994, UN Doc. CAT/C/13/ D/15/1994.

"... the Committee recommends that further steps be taken to ensure the effective implementation of the Convention[on the Rights of the Child] ... the Committee also wishes to emphasise the importance of taking action to ensure that the general principles of the Convention, particularly those relating to non-discrimination, the best interests of the child and the respect for the views of the child as guaranteed under articles 2, 3, and 12 respectively, are reflected in domestic law. With regard to article 12 ... it is recommended that children be provided with the opportunity to be heard in judicial and administrative proceedings."

" ... Solutions should also be sought to avoid expulsions causing the separation of families, in the spirit of article 9 of the Convention. More generally, the Committee recommends that the Government address the situation of unaccompanied children and children having been refused refugee status and awaiting deportation in the light of the Convention's provisions ..." [218]

This set the stage for the Baker case in 1999 where children's rights were not given effect and the Supreme Court failed to hear the case of the children themselves.

In late November 1993 and early 1994 the UN Human Rights Committee gave its views on extradition to the death penalty in Kindler and Ng respectively. Aspects of the CCPR article 6 right to life, due process in the death penalty, and aspects of CCPR article 7, no torture or cruel

---

[218] Concluding observations of the Committee on the Rights of the Child : Canada. 20/06/95. CRC/C/15/Add.37, at paras 23 and 24 respectively.

or inhuman treatment or punishment, were at issue in extradition to the death penalty. Although this followed the Supreme Court of Canada cases, it confirmed the view in international human rights first set out by the European Court of Human Rights in 1989.

The cases in the next chapter fall one before and one after the 1999 examination of Canada by the UN Human Rights Committee which expressed the following concerns and recommendations:

> "The Committee is concerned with the inadequacy of remedies for violations of articles 2 [giving effect to and ensuring rights], 3 [ensuring an effective remedy] and 26 [non discrimination and equal treatment] of the Covenant. The Committee recommends that the relevant human rights legislation be amended so as to guarantee access to a competent tribunal and to an effective remedy in all cases of discrimination." [219]
>
> "The Committee is concerned that gaps remain between the protection of rights under the Canadian charter and other federal and provincial laws and the protection required under the Covenant, and recommends measures to ensure full implementation of Covenant rights. In this regard the Committee recommends that consideration be given to the establishment of a public body responsible for overseeing implementation of the Covenant and for reporting on any deficiencies." [220]

---

[219] Concluding observations of the Human Rights Committee : Canada. 07/04/99. CCPR/C/79/Add.105, para. 9.

[220] *Ibid* para. 10.

The Standing Senate Committee on Human Rights has the possibility of become the public body envisaged, but it has no real authority to overseeing the implementation of the Covenant. The HRC continued:

> "The Committee is concerned that Canada takes the position that compelling security interests may be invoked to justify the removal of aliens to countries where they may face a substantial risk of torture or cruel, inhuman or degrading treatment. The Committee refers to its General Comment on article 7 and recommends that Canada revise this policy in order to comply with the requirements of article 7 and to meet its obligation never to expel, extradite, deport or otherwise remove a person to a place where treatment or punishment that is contrary to article 7 is a substantial risk."[221]

This was exactly the situation in the Suresh case. I attended this HRC examination of Canada in New York with lawyer Barbara Jackman and I know that several members were shown the Federal Court of Appeal decision just prior to the examination. As we shall see, the Supreme Court subsequently ignored and defied this international obligation. The Committee continued:

> "The Committee remains concerned about Canada's policy in relation to expulsion of long-term alien residents, without giving full consideration in all cases to the protection of all Covenant rights, in particular under articles 23 [protecting the family] and 24 [special rights of the child]."[222]

---

[221] *Ibid* para. 13.
[222] *Ibid* para.15.

These rights were at issue in the Baker case which we shall consider in the next chapter.

The change at the Human Rights Committee from the early days of the *Charter* is dramatic. The expectation in the 1984 examination of Canada was that the *Charter* gave effect to CCPR rights for everyone. In 1999, almost two decades later, Canada is being explicitly urged to give effect to fundamental CCPR rights as these effect extradition and expulsion.

In 1992, the Canadian Council of Churches had put its defeated court action before the Inter-American Commission on Human Rights and facilitated individual complaints. The Inter-American Commission on Human Rights held a General Hearing in Washington D.C. in 1996 and then undertook an On Site Visit to Canada in 1997. The visit included discussions by members of the Inter-American Commission with Canadian officials and judges as well as with NGOs, refugees and other non-citizens in public hearings in Toronto, Ottawa and Montreal. Commission members visited jails and talked to individuals detained. Thus, it is reasonable to suppose that the Supreme Court was aware of the international obligations after 1997 and certainly by 1999, the time of decisions on the next two cases to be discussed. As we shall see, the Supreme Court responded by creating an appearance of progressive generosity while doing nothing significant to ensure the CCPR rights or to ensure an effective court remedy for the individual compatible with American Declaration of Rights and Duties of Man article XVIII.

5. Saving Some Face in the late 1990s

The Pushpanathan decision of the Supreme Court in 1998 is widely viewed as a major contribution to refugee rights – and it is. The *Baker* case is seen as a landmark case allowing international rights to play a role in Canadian law. In a sense it was. Yet decisions like *Pushpanathan* and *Baker* seem less satisfactory when measured against the international obligations. Even the elements viewed as positive and giving effect to rights can be elements where it is convenient for the court to give effect to rights. There had been steadily growing concerns by the UN treaty bodies about international rights at issue in expulsion. Yet the *Pushpanathan* and *Baker* decisions did little to change this.

Pushpanathan 1998

In 1985, Veluppillai Pushpanathan claimed refugee status, but the claim was never heard because he was given residence status in Canada under another procedure.[223] He was subsequently charged with conspiracy to traffic in a narcotic, pleaded guilty and was sentenced to eight years in prison. In 1991, when on parole, he renewed his claim for Convention refugee status. The government issued a deportation order conditional on finding him not to be a Convention refugee. The Immigration and Refugee Board, IRB, found Pushpanathan was not a refugee by virtue of an "exclusion clause" in the refugee definition, article 1F(c) of the of the 1951 Convention Relating to the Status of Refugees. It says that the Convention does not apply to a person who "has been guilty of acts contrary to the purposes and principles of the United Nations".

---

[223] *Pushpanathan v. Canada* [1998] 1 S.C.R. 982

Pushpanathan appealed. The Federal Court, Trial Division dismissed his request for judicial review but certified a question for the Federal Court of Appeal. Was it a mistake to interpret the Convention definition so as to deny refugee status to a person guilty of a serious narcotic offence? The Federal Court of Appeal said "no", but the case was appealed to the Supreme Court.

The Canadian Council of Churches did not itself intervene before the Supreme Court. However, the Canadian Council of Refugees successfully sought leave to intervene. The primary concern was to give effect to the persuasive soft law from the Executive Committee of the UN high Commissioner for Refugees about article 1F(c). The CCC missed the opportunity to press for a more meaningful appeal.

In its decision, the Supreme Court noted that the 1951 Convention had a "human rights character", that the purpose of the subsection of the refugee definition was to deny status to people "responsible for serious, sustained or systemic violations of fundamental human rights which amount to persecution in a non-war setting". The Court found that "exclusion", article 1F(c), applies when international law has determined that particular acts are such serious and sustained violations of fundamental human rights as to amount to persecution, or are explicitly recognized as contrary to the UN purposes and principles by accepted international agreement, by explicit UN resolution or are acts which a court can itself characterize as serious, sustained and systemic violations of fundamental human rights constituting persecution.

> "Conspiring to traffic in a narcotic is not a violation of Art.1F(c). Even though international trafficking in drugs is an extremely serious problem,

> individuals should not be deprived of the essential
> protections contained in the Convention for having
> committed those acts."[224]

Pushpanathan's appeal was allowed. This ruling made a positive contribution to refugee law that can be applauded. However, the obligation to ensure international rights sets a harsh test for a court.

Unfortunately, the Supreme Court only went so far as to say that the standard for judicial review was flexible. A standard of "correctness" applied to points of law in the juridical review of an IRB decision. This was in the direction of international obligations, but the Court ruled that the outcome need not be "correct" and gave no weight to the consequence for the individual of the decision being reviewed. The review standard is the same whether the consequence is jail in Canada or deportation to a real risk of torture. This judicial review need not ensure an effective judicial remedy for the individual whose fundamental rights are threatened by acts of the authorities. Efforts to improve this part of the decision feature in subsequent Canadian Council of Churches interventions in *Baker* and *Suresh*.

Dissenting Justices Cory and Major captured a sense of CAT Art.3 and the international perspective on safeguards from a risk of torture at the end of an otherwise mistaken dissent. They first argue that the evolving context of UN opposition to drug trafficking qualifies for interpreting the 1951 Convention Art. 1F(c). This dissenting argument draws on the principle for treaty interpretation that the treaty is to be interpreted in its current juridical context – a principle which I have shown in chapter 2 is correct.

---

[224] *Pushpanathan, Op.Cit.,* Summary of Judgment.

However, the juridical context must be that of the treaty provision. The majority of justices gave effect to the ordinary meaning of Art. 1F(c) in the context of its treaty text, as well as of the *traveaux preparatoires*.[225] They draw on "soft law" - the UNHCR Handbook, approved by the Executive Committee of the UN High Commissioner for Refugees.[226] These require a restrictive approach to the application of 1951 Convention Art. 1F(c). For me, as for the majority, it is the text in its treaty context and the directly related "soft law" which are the relevant juridical context. The UNHCR and its Executive Committee of governments are linked to the application of this treaty and to the international interpretation of article 1. The dissenters had to themselves suppose a link between general UN statements concerning narcotics and this particular article 1F(c).

However, the comments of the dissenting justices about due process in deportation give some effect to other international treaty obligations which the majority missed. Their dissenting comment comes close to the subsequent Concluding Observations by the Committee against Torture in 2005, set out later in this chapter. Cory j. and Major j. found that following and ensuring the principles of natural justice was required for any deportation to real risk of torture:

> "... there must be an opportunity for a hearing ... and the hearing must comply with all the principles of natural justice. As well, the individual ... ought to be entitled to have the decision reviewed to ensure that it did indeed comply with those principles."[227]

---

[225] *Ibid* para. 56-61.
[226] *Ibid* para. 53.
[227] *Ibid* para. 157.

The Canadian Council of Churches later quoted this reasoning in its *Suresh* intervention.

For the world of refugee affairs *Pushpanathan* was a significant advance. The international test was met in some parts of the judgment. The Supreme Court gave effect to an aspect of an international Convention, article 1 of the 1951 Convention Relating to the Status of Refugees. This article of this treaty is in Canadian law, and is quoted in part in the *Immigration Act*. The Court said the 1951 Convention had a human rights quality. The Court provided a remedy by referring *Pushpanathan* back for another refugee hearing before the same tribunal. This hardly ensures protection. The international obligations are not only those about the right to seek asylum, American Declaration Art. XXVII. The right to seek asylum then attracts the American Declaration Art. XVIII right to have a court ensure respect for this right and, further, the right to a simple effective court remedy capable of protecting the individual from acts of the authorities which might violate this right. In theory, Canadian law's "leave" and other access provisions might be interpreted so as to ensure a full court review of the adjudication of the right to seek asylum – a right engaged by application of the refugee definition.

For the majority of the Supreme Court, the ultimate question for judicial review was what the legislature intended, not what the *Charter* required when interpreted so as to give effect to international rights obligations. The *Immigration Act* was the primary reference. Yet the "soft law" of the Executive Committee of the UN High Commissioner for Refugees has long set out a formal reconsideration of a negative refugee status decision as an obligation. The Report by the Inter-American Commission on Human Rights that subsequently appeared in 2000 argued that ensuring a reconsideration or appeal on the merits after any refugee hearing, not just after Pushpanathan's, is part of the due process obligations of the American Declaration:

> "...Given that even the best decision-makers may err in passing judgment, and given the potential risk to life which may result from such an error, an appeal on the merits of a negative determination constitutes a necessary element of international protection..."[228]

Beyond the appeal on the merits, the Commission was concerned about the leave provision, the prerequisite for judicial review by a court. Then in 2005, the Committee against Torture implied related concerns and offered advice when probability of torture is at issue:

> "... the State party [Canada] should provide for judicial review of the merits, rather than simply of the reasonableness, of decisions to expel an individual where there are substantial grounds to believe the person faces a risk of torture ..."[229]

We might recall at this point that in *Singh et al* Beetz j. had noted that at least [my underline] one oral hearing was required to satisfy the *Charter* rights.

---

[228] Inter-American Commission 2000 Report, *Op.Cit.* para. 109.
[229] Committee against Torture, "Conclusions and Recommendations ... Canada," UN Doc. CAT/C/CO/34/CAN, May 2005, Para.5(f).

Baker 1999

After the CRC report in 1995 and the HRC report on Canada in 1999, the Baker case was a chance for the Supreme Court to close the gap on family and children's rights. Others have written in far greater detail about *Baker* and other Canadian case law concerning children's rights.[230] Here I focus on the test and the CCC intervention. The facts for *Baker* are set out in the case.[231] Mavis Baker was a non-citizen single mother with Canadian dependent children who had lived and worked in Canada for several years without formal status. She was ordered deported because she lacked formal immigration status to remain. She applied for an exemption, based on humanitarian and compassionate considerations under the *Immigration Act*. This application was supported by letters of concern about the non-availability of medical treatment for her health condition in her country of origin and the effect of her possible departure on her Canadian citizen children. A senior immigration officer wrote a reply to Mavis Baker saying there were insufficient reasons to warrant processing her application in Canada. His letter contained no reasons for the decision. Her lawyer was able to obtain the notes made by the investigating officer and used by the senior officer in making his decision. The officer was "dismissive" of any interests of the children.

---

[230] Aiken and Scott, *Op.Cit.2000*.

[231] *Baker* v. *Canada*, [1999] 2 S.C.R. 817.

The Federal Court Trial Division, dismissed an application for judicial review but certified a question for review at the Federal Court of Appeal: "Given that the Immigration Act does not expressly incorporate the language of Canada's international obligations with respect to the International Convention on the Rights of the Child, must federal immigration authorities treat the best interests of the child as a primary consideration in assessing an applicant under section 114(2) of the Immigration Act?"

International family and children's rights were clearly at issue. Under the then *Immigration Act* an administrative decision could be reviewed with leave by the Federal Court. Requesting an appeal of the humanitarian application, H&C, was a means to get the rights involved in expulsion before a court. The HRC had made plain that CCPR article 17 and 23 family rights could be at issue in expulsion in its 1993 *Stewart v. Canada* and 1994 *Canepa v. Canada* cases, even though no violation was found in those case circumstances. The Inter-American Commission on Human Rights case, *Joseph v. Canada*, is an example of a case which was lost on the matter of standing, but which nonetheless, allowed the Inter-American Commission to provide views on Canada's obligations. In this case, the rights to asylum and family and children's rights were determined to be at issue.[232]

Mavis Baker was able to be heard before the Supreme Court on account of a charitable intervention by the Canadian Council of Churches. Initially, she had been

---

[232] In the Joseph case report the Inter-American Commission showed the American Declaration right to seek and obtain asylum applied to Canada's refugee procedures. Canada implicitly accepted the right of the Commission to note and consider other related treaty rights binding on Canada. IACHR *Joseph Case, Op. Cit. 1993.*

denied legal aid to seek leave to appeal to the Supreme Court. The Council funded her submission requesting leave of the Supreme Court to be heard. Once leave was granted, the legal aid plan was willing to provide funding.[233] This need for charitable intervention raises questions about the Supreme Court assumption in *Canadian Council of Churches* v. *M.E.I.* (1992) that individuals could easily raise Constitutional issues before it themselves.[234]

At the time of the *Mavis Baker* case, the case law of the Federal Court of Appeal had taken the position that the separation of parents from Canadian citizen children by deportation of the parents was a private matter of no concern to a State. Such a deportation, said the Federal Court, was without rights implications. The child has no right at issue in the deportation of its parents.[235] At the

---

[233] The author notes that Ontario Legal Aid subsequently allowed the Canadian Council of Churches to recover the costs that it had paid in order to allow Mavis Baker seek leave to appeal.

[234] Tom Clark, 16 *Windsor Yearbook of Access to Justice* 218, 1998, 226. The author notes that to the credit of the Ontario Legal Aid Program, it refunded the Canadian Council of Churches these costs when the Supreme Court agreed to hear the case.

[235] *Ewa Pawlack J Langner et al* v. *M.E.I.*, Federal Court of Appeal A-386-94, Judgement March 21, 1995, "The *Canadian Charter of Rights and Freedoms* can have no application in this case. The appellant parents' decision to take their children to Poland with them or to leave them with family members living in Canada is a decision which is their own ... The Canadian government has nothing to do with this decision ... The appellant children's rights and freedoms, which attach to their Canadian citizenship ... are not at issue ... There is no threat to the children's right to life, liberty and security ... Moreover, a child has no constitutional right never to be separated from its parents ... a child's right is to be where its best interests require it to be ... Even if these international obligations [Convention on the Rights of the Child] had been incorporated into Canada's domestic law ... we need only look to articles 9 and 10 ... to find ... arguments are entirely devoid of merit."

same time, international case law recognized family rights as at issue in deportation. The European Court of Human Rights had established that such deportations would normally be considered a disproportionate limitation of family rights under the European Convention even when those to be deported had a record of criminal conviction.[236] With family rights and children's rights so clearly at issue, *Charter* rights should have given full effect to these international rights for non-citizens.

The Canadian Council of Churches intervened in *Baker* to address "the nature of Canada's obligation through its domestic laws ... to ensure that there are domestic remedies which are meaningful effective and fair available to persons claiming a human rights breach."[237] As the Inter-American Commission would also subsequently point out, the Council argued:

> "the right to an effective remedy is an independent and separate right fundamental to the protection of other human rights."[238]

The Council pointed to *Charter s.24(1)* as the effective remedy required in Canadian law. The Council characterized the issue as "whether Canada is obligated to consider the liberty interests of a non-resident parent and Canadian children, and in the context of this consideration, the best interests of the child and, if so obligated, whether the consequences caused by the Appellant's removal

---

See also Aiken and Scott, *Op.Cit. 2000*, 214.

[236] See *Moustaquim* v. *Belgium, Op.Cit.*.

[237] Canadian Council of Churches, Factum of the Intervenor, Mavis Baker v. MEI, SCC File no. 25823, para. 3.

[238] *Ibid* para.8.

warrant stricter procedural safeguards."[239] The Council enumerated elements of an effective remedy:

- recognizing that the liberty and or security interest of Baker and her children are engaged;
- ensuring an independent and impartial decision maker;
- hearing the child and parents with an oral hearing if credibility is at issue (CRC art.12);
- giving reasons;
- having courts ensure respect by state actors for the human rights of the individuals who come before them.

The Council continued:

> "human rights entitlement is an indicator of the degree of scrutiny which a court must apply on review ... human rights disentitlement mandates the highest degree of scrutiny ... which may include both an analysis of law and fact".[240]

The Council argued that its view was consistent with international obligations. The reader can decide that for him or herself at this point.

Charter rights and international obligations were put before the Court including CCPR Art.17 & 23 family rights, CRC Art.9 right of children to maintain relations and contact with both parents and the CRC Art.10 the right to leave and return for reunion and maintaining parent-child relationships. The CRC rights inform the CCPR Art.24 special rights of the child. These were the very rights raised

---

[239] *Ibid* para. 23.
[240] *Ibid* para. 25-26.

as concerns by the treaty bodies and set out at the end of the last chapter. The Council suggested a way in which the Court could have complied. The Supreme Court failed to apply the *Charter*. Thus the Court also failed to give effect to international family and children's rights at issue through a "liberty interest" under *Charter* s.7. The Court chose to give effect to only the principle in CRC, Art.3 - the best interests of the child. The Court required that this principle become one factor in discretionary administrative decision-making under the *Immigration Act*.

As Aiken and Scott note, the CCC intervention had attempted to nuance and so correct the Supreme Court's approach in *Chiarelli* by suggesting that the scope of rights might vary according to immigration status, but that the existence and protection of fundamental rights went beyond immigration status.[241] The Court ignored this advice.[242] The Court again accepted the scheme of the *Immigration Act (1976)* as Constitutional, but it did so now in a new and different context. This new humanitarian context contrasted sharply with the context of criminality and public danger of *Chiarelli*. In *Baker* the Court chose to insulate entry and remaining issues from the supreme law of Canada even when national security and criminality were no longer at issue.

Some might point out that *Charter* rights had not been raised in the lower courts in this *Baker* case. Such a precondition had been a pattern followed by the Supreme Court in the later 1990s. However, the Supreme Court is supreme. It can set limits for its own role. It can choose to avoid aspects of its constitutional role or not. The fact remains, the court did not apply the *Charter*. It failed to

---

[241] See Aiken and Scott, *Op.Cit. 2000*, 223.
[242] *Baker, Op. Cit. 1999* para. 39-47.

implement Canada's obligation to respect, give effect to and ensure international rights by failing to apply *Charter* rights.

The Supreme Court was the only organ of the State in a position to ensure the right to an effective judicial remedy for *Baker* who was facing deportation and separation from her child as a consequence of acts of authority. The Court failed its obligation to ensure an effective judicial remedy for her. Instead, the Court required minimal reasons for an administrative decision. It itself accepted scribbled notes. It made small changes to the nature of judicial review.[243] The result of all the Supreme Court energy was that Mavis Baker was sent to another official to face wide administrative discretion once more. The ruling in *Baker* means that one rather vague principle from one international Convention ratified ten years before – best interest of the child - should play a role as a factor in administrative decision-making. This does not warrant much praise for ensuring international rights.

Justice Iacobucci made an intriguing observation that the majority decision could have been different had it been based on the Charter:

> "the result may well have been different had my colleague concluded that the appellant's claim fell within the ambit of rights protected by the Canadian Charter of Rights and Freedoms. Had this been the case, the Court would have had an opportunity to consider the application of the

---

[243] An immigration official subsequently told the author that since the Supreme Court had accepted scribbled notes made available by an immigration official on request as "reasons", they were sufficient as reasons.

interpretive presumption, established by the Court's decision in Slaight Communications Inc. v. Davidson, [1989] 1 S.C.R. 1038, and confirmed in subsequent jurisprudence, that administrative discretion involving Charter rights be exercised in accordance with similar international human rights norms."

However, the observation was small comfort to interveners like the Canadian Council of Churches that had in fact put *Charter* issues and arguments before a Court which, in theory, could have stepped outside its self imposed procedural constraints to consider them.

The Council of Churches has reason to view the decision with some cynicism. In *Canadian Council of Churches* v. *MEI* the Court told the Council that its appropriate role was intervener. When the Council presented *Charter* rights issues ten years later as intervener in *Baker,* the Court ignored the issues again.

Moreover, the Court did not choose to hear the subsequent case of *Francis* in which *Charter* rights and international family and children's rights had been raised in the lower courts. The government discreetly settled the Francis case. The Supreme Court then ruled that the case and the issues were moot.[244] [245] This behaviour cannot be described as giving effect to or ensuring international rights.

---

[244] The Supreme Court had granted leave for an appeal of the Francis case. The CCC had hoped to intervene. Then one presumes that the government offered to grant status in return for no publicity. The CCC wrote the Court urging it to continue to hear the case since the issues were evidently important. The Court found the case moot.

[245] Aiken and Scott, *Op.Cit. 2000,* 248-250.

That CCPR rights were at issue to be given effect by the *Charter* became even clearer in international case law of the binding treaties after *Baker*. Previously, the Human Rights Committee had given effect to the CCPR article 17 right as at issue as in deportations of *Stewart v Canada* and *Canepa v. Canada*, but it had avoided finding the State in violation of these CCPR rights. In the rather special circumstances of *Winata* v. *Australia* the HRC subsequently found that deporting parents with a citizen child violated a combination of CCPR Art. 17, 23 and 24.[246]

The 2000 Report by the Inter-American Commission on Human Rights makes note of the *Baker* case as a positive contribution. The Commission nonetheless "finds it pertinent to offer a few observations about what is required in terms of the rights of the child and to family life" noting that American Declaration articles V and VI "prohibit arbitrary or illegal interference with family life" and that article VII requires special measures for children. After noting the relevance of CCPR Art.24, CRC Art. 3, 9 12, and the advice of the UN Committee on the Rights of the Child, the Inter-American Commission on Human Rights concluded:

> "Given the nature of articles V, VI and VII ... interpreted in relation to Canada's obligations under the Convention on the Rights of the Child, where decision-making involves the potential separation of a family, the resulting interference with family life may only be justified where necessary to meet a pressing need to protect public order, and where the means are proportional to that

---

[246] Human Rights Committee, *Winata* v. *Australia*, Communication 930/2000, Views 16 August 2001, UN Doc. CCPR/C/72/D/930/2000.

end.".[247]

Deportation of parents with citizen children would be a permissible limitation of the rights involved only in exceptional circumstances.[248] In Canada, *Bill of Rights* s.2(e) due process should apply for the adjudication of any rights in federal matters. There is also the international right to an effective judicial remedy if acts of authority would threaten family or children's rights.

The court did not ensure the right to an effective judicial remedy. My international test was not met. The Court made some changes in the level of evidence needed for the "leave" to get judicial review of an administrative decision. That was helpful but inadequate.

Questions about a high threshold for the leave test at the Federal Court had been raised and evaded in an earlier Supreme Court case discussed above, *Reza*, where the right to *Habeas Corpus* was at issue. In *Baker* the Court talked of its flexible pragmatic approach to the test standard. As in *Chiarelli*, what the federal parliament intended remained the starting point. The starting point was not the *Charter* plus the international obligation to protect rights. Non-citizens got no appeal as of right when important rights of children and family rights are at issue in a deportation.

The lower courts did with this decision what the Supreme Court provided for. Judicial reviews continued to require a leave only on points of law to access a court. There is still no appeal on the merits. However, after *Mavis Baker,* non-citizens only needed to show that they had a "reasonable case" on points of law to have access to judicial review on

---

[247] Inter-American Commission 2000 Report, *Op.Cit.*, para. 161 - 166.
[248] *Ibid* para. 166.

any points of law at issue.

Summary of International Advice 2000

In 2000, the Inter-American Commission on Human Rights issued its Report on the Situation of Human Rights of Asylum Seekers within the Canadian Refugee Determination System. The Report offers all OAS member States an authoritative interpretation of the American Declaration and other human rights treaties having effect for asylum seekers in the Americas. The report also offers particular advice about international obligations for Canada.

Surprisingly, as of December 2004 the Report had not been posted with other international human rights jurisprudence on the web site of Heritage Canada. The proposed new legislation, *Immigration and Refugee protection Act 2002*, appeared so shortly after the release of the report that it could not have taken into account the recommendations. Although *IRPA 2002* did propose a form of appeal on the merits after a negative refugee status hearing - a provision of *IRPA 2002* which has never been implemented.

Quotations from Inter American Commission 2000 Report occur before and after this point. Here, it seems useful to summarize and repeat the key issues:

- the obligation to "respect and ensure the fundamental rights" of all persons subject to their jurisdiction. The fundamental rights are the rights in the American Declaration. (Para. 31 and 31.)

- with respect to finding persons ineligible for a

refugee status hearing, the right to seek asylum requires that a claimant be heard in presenting the application. (Para. 58, 64 and 68-70.)

- allowing the determination process to be reopened for new facts or evidence would provide an important safeguard. (Para 73.)

- measures to enable prompter refugee family reunion would be consistent with the right to family life. (Para. 78.)

- with respect to the provision requiring leave for judicial review, "the right of access to judicial protection to ensure respect for a legal right requires available and effective recourse for the violation of a right protected under the Declaration or the Constitution ..." (Para. 95.) Controls on that right must further a legitimate objective and the means must be reasonable and proportionate. (Para. 99.)

- with respect to an appeal from a negative refugee status decision, "existing judicial and administrative review mechanisms may provide important protections ... but do not bridge the gap resulting from the absence of a merits-based review." (Para. 115.)

- with respect to pre-deportation administrative review to ensure no expulsion to a real risk of torture, freedom from torture is an essential aspect of personal security under American Declaration article I, and all persons must have access to any such pre-deportation review. (Para. 118-122.)

- with respect to access to review of legality of detention, article XXV requires judicial review without delay, period review is necessary because with time preventive detention results in an increasing burden on the rights of the person deprived of liberty. When the burden becomes too great, continuing may no longer be justified. (Para. 137 and 142.)

- with respect to "the security certificate regime", the certificate review process does not provide prompt judicial oversight of the decision to detain required by American Declaration article XXV, and a delay of 4 or 8 months exceeds the requirement for "promptly", and further, "it is a fundamental principle of due process that the parties engaged in the judicial determination of rights and duties must enjoy equality of arms," a person subject of secret evidence will not enjoy a full opportunity. (Para. 148, 151, 157.)

- with respect to family and children's rights and the Baker case, "Given the nature of articles V, VI and VII of the American Declaration, interpreted in relation to ... the Convention on the Rights of the Child, where decision-making involves the potential separation of a family, the resulting interference with family life may only be justified where necessary to meet a pressing need to protect public order and where the means are proportional ..." (Para. 161, 166.)

Towards the end of 2000, more concerns about immigration procedures came from the UN Committee against Torture in the Conclusions and Recommendations after its examination of Canada:

> "The public danger risk assessment [Security Certificate procedure], without interview or transparency, is carried out prior to the refugee determination procedure, and, if a person is considered a security risk, this person is not eligible to have his case examined in-depth under the normal refugee determination procedure. In addition, the Committee notes that at present both the review of security risk and the review of the existence of humanitarian and compassionate grounds are determined by the same governmental body [at the time, immigration officials]; the Committee is also concerned that the alleged lack of independence of decision-makers, as well as the possibility that a person can be removed while an application for humanitarian review is underway, may constitute obstacles to the effectiveness of the remedies to protect the rights in article 3(1) of the Convention;" [249]

Here the Committee took aim at the Security Certificate regime which had applied in *Chiarelli* and which would return in the cases of *Suresh* and *Ahani*. This concern reinforced the criticism from the Inter-American Commission on human Rights, above. The Committee against Torture also took aim at the Canadian administrative procedures that allegedly give effect to the

---

[249] "Conclusions and Recommendations of the Committee against Torture: Canada" , UN Doc. CAT/C/XXV/Concl.4, 22 November 2000, para. 5(f), the [] are the author's. See also the Recommendation 6(b).

CAT Art.3 right to protection from expulsion to a serious probability of torture - the Humanitarian and Compassionate procedure and at the pre removal risk assessment procedure. There is a reference to the fact that there is no automatic stay for prevention of deportation while a person's request for permission for judicial review is before the Federal Court. This concern reinforces the concern of the Inter-American Commission, above.

Of course, the above CAT advice appeared after the Supreme Court decision on *Baker*. Moreover, *Baker* was a case which involved family and children's rights, due process, judicial protection and the Humanitarian and Compassionate procedure. However, the CAT and the Commission reports were available before the decisions on *Burns*, *Suresh* and *Ahani*. As we shall find, the concerns of the UN Committee against Torture remain and were repeated when considering the admissibility of the case *Enrique Falcon Rios* v. *Canada* in late 2004.[250] So in the refugee cases of *Suresh* and *Ahani*, the Supreme Court had an opportunity to consider clear statements about Canada's international obligations to ensure court protection of rights, to ensure access to judicial protection, to provide court review of the legality of detention without delay, and to ensure that due process includes equality of arms within the security certificate regime.

---

[250] Committee against Torture, *Enrique Falcon Rios* v. *Canada*, Communication No 133/1999, Views 6 December 2004, UN Doc. CAT/C/32/DR/133/1999/Rev.1, para. 7.3 & 7.5.

6. Into the 21ˢᵗ Century

The Supreme Court failed to give effect to international rights via the *Charter* in *Chiarelli*. In the early 1990s, some avoidance of international rights might have been justifiable. The international treaty bodies had been reluctant to find violations of rights in the early individual cases involving non-citizens and expulsion that began coming from countries like Canada and Sweden. There was little international case law with detailed reasoning about expulsion before 1989. By the end of the 20ᵗʰ century, UN case law had become better reasoned and more consistent with the international yardstick obligations that one could have deduced from the beginning. By 2000 there was clearly a gap between Canadian law in expulsion of non citizens and UN case law. In addition, there was now an explicit gap between the American Declaration human rights obligations as well. The cases of *Burns* and *Suresh* provided Canadian courts with opportunities to deal with some concerns of the UN treaty bodies and offered opportunities for the obligations under the American Declaration of Rights and Duties of Man.

Burns in 2001

Ten years after the extradition case law established by *Kinder* and *Ng*, the Supreme Court faced another proposed extradition case: that of Burns and Rafay.²⁵¹ The father, mother and sister of Rafay were found bludgeoned to death in their home in Bellevue, Washington, in July 1994. Burns and Rafay, who had been friends at high school in British Columbia, were at the Rafay home on the night of the murders. If the confessions subsequently made to

---

²⁵¹ *United States* v. *Burns*, [2001] 1 S.C.R. 283.

undercover RCMP officers are true, the three members of the Rafay family were bludgeoned to death by Burns while Rafay watched. The Bellevue police did not have enough evidence to charge them. When they returned to Canada, the RCMP initiated an elaborate undercover operation to elicit confessions. They were arrested in British Columbia and jailed for extradition pending the decision of the Minister of Justice. The Minister signed an Order for Surrender to extradite them to the State of Washington without assurances in respect of the death penalty.

Rafay and Burns had sent arguments to the Minister saying *inter alia* the Minister was required by *Charter* ss. 6(1) [freedom of movement], 7 [life liberty and security unless taken by due process], and 12 [prohibition of cruel treatment] to seek assurances that the death penalty would not be used by the US. They argued that unconditional extradition to the death penalty would "shock the Canadian conscience" because they were 18 years old at the time of the offence and they were citizens of Canada. The Minister argued that the factors outlined in the earlier Supreme Court *Kindler* extradition case did not require assurances. The age, although "youthful", qualified them as adults in the Canadian criminal system. Citizenship was not itself a "special circumstance" to allow escape from sentencing in the United States where murders were committed. Canada should not permit itself to become a safe haven for persons seeking to escape justice.

The British Columbia Court of Appeal set aside the Minister's decision and directed the Minister to seek the assurances. The BC Court noted that if put to death in Washington, they would not be able to use the right of return under s. 6(1) of the *Charter*. The *Kindler* analysis was not relevant to Canadian citizens facing the death penalty. With regard to ss. 7 and 12 of the *Charter*, the BC

Court turned to the Supreme Court's decisions in *Kindler* and *Ng* and decided these did not help *Burns* and *Rafay* since they applied to citizens and non-citizens alike. The BC Court ruled that not only was s. 6(1) of the *Charter* violated by the unconditional surrender, but as a matter of administrative law, the Minister was required to determine in each case what is appropriate having regard to the circumstances. The Minister should have placed more weight on the young age and citizenship before signing the extradition order. The Supreme Court judgment said:

> "Section 12 of the *Charter* guarantees ... the right not to be subjected to any cruel and unusual treatment or punishment ..."[252]
> " ... The *Charter* only guarantees certain rights and freedoms from infringement by the Parliament and government of Canada ... and ... the legislature and government of each province. There can be no doubt that the actions undertaken by the Government of Canada in extradition ... are subject to scrutiny under the *Charter* (s. 32). Equally, though, there cannot be any doubt that the *Charter* does not govern the actions of a foreign country ... In particular the *Charter* cannot be given extraterritorial effect to govern how criminal proceedings in a foreign country are to be conducted."[253]

However, the *Charter* is a means for meeting Canada's obligations to ensure fundamental rights when there is a real possibility these rights would be subsequently violated as a consequence of an act by Canada such as expulsion. As the Court notes:

---

[252] *Ibid* para. 50.
[253] *Ibid* para. 51.

"Nevertheless, counsel for the respondents suggests that Canada cannot avoid shouldering responsibility for the imposition of the death penalty just because it would be a foreign government, if anyone, that puts the respondents to death. ...There is some support for this view in the decision of the European Court of Human Rights in *Soering* : In sum, the decision ... to extradite a fugitive may give rise to an issue under Article 3 [of the *Convention for the Protection of Human Rights and Fundamental Freedoms*, which relates to section 12 of the *Charter*], and hence engage the responsibility of that State under the Convention, where substantial grounds have been shown for believing that the person concerned, if extradited, faces a real risk of being subjected to torture or to inhuman or degrading treatment or punishment in the requesting country."[254]

Canada has not ratified the European Convention. It has ratified the CCPR and it has ratified the UN Convention against Torture. Yet there is no reference here to the binding obligation of the Convention against Torture Art.3, the prohibition of extradition when there is a serious probability of torture, or to the binding obligation to ensure, in expulsion situations, the right to protection from torture or cruel treatment, CCPR Art.7 taken with CCPR Art. 2. The Supreme Court notes:

"The 'responsibility of the State' is certainly engaged under the *Charter* by a ministerial decision to extradite without assurances. While the Canadian government would not itself inflict capital

---

[254] *Ibid* para. 52-53.

punishment, its decision to extradite without assurances would be a necessary link in the chain of causation to that *potential* result. The question is whether the linkage is strong enough and direct enough to invoke s. 12 in an extradition proceeding, especially where, as here, there are many potential outcomes other than capital punishment. The view previously taken by this Court is that the proper place for the 'state responsibility' debate is under s. 7. We affirm the correctness of that approach.".[255]

Once again, the Court did not ensure the right to an effective judicial remedy capable of protecting the substantive rights from acts of authority such as ministerial decision making. The Court noted that the "responsibility of the State" is engaged by a Ministerial decision. Surprisingly, the Court did not seem aware that the same responsibility of the State vis a vis international rights obligations might be engaged by its own decision. The Supreme Court left intact its earlier *Kindler* endorsement of the Minister's "broad discretion" under the Extradition Act, but it now recognized some Constitutional role:

> "While constitutionally valid, the Minister's discretion is limited by the *Charter*. ... Although it is generally for the Minister, not the court, to assess the weight of competing considerations ... Death penalty cases are uniquely bound up with basic constitutional values and the court is the guardian of the Constitution." [256]

Section 6 of the *Charter* on freedom of movement, as it applies to citizens, was before the Court. The Court said:

---

[255] *Ibid* para. 54-55.
[256] *Ibid* Opening Summary of Judgment.

> " ... extradition is a prima facie infringement of the
> s. 6(1) right of every Canadian citizen to "remain in"
> Canada ... The respondents will not, on this
> occasion, leave their homeland willingly. Their
> forcible removal must be justified under s. 1 of the
> Charter."[257] (para. 41)

The Court missed the opportunity to "protect and ensure"
or "give effect" to the international right which also applies
to non-citizens, CCPR article 12. The reference to s.1 here is
helpful, but the Court did not apply it. The Court
continued:

> "As the s. 1 justification for a breach of s. 6(1)
> parallels that for a breach of s. 7 in any event, a
> more ample discussion of the s. 1 arguments will be
> deferred until s. 7 has been considered." [258]

Similarly, the Court did not fully adjudicate or give effect to
the CCPR Art.7 right to protection from torture or cruel
and unusual treatment or punishment which had by now
been determined internationally to be involved in death
penalty cases.

> "... the degree of causal remoteness between the
> extradition order to face trial and the potential
> imposition of capital punishment as one of many
> possible outcomes to this prosecution make this a
> case more appropriately reviewed under s. 7 than
> under s. 12. ..."[259]

---

[257] *Ibid* para. 41.
[258] *Ibid* para. 49.
[259] *Ibid* para. 57.

> "We are not called upon ... to determine whether
> capital punishment would, if authorized by the
> Canadian Parliament, violate s. 12 of the *Charter*
> ("cruel and unusual treatment or punishment"),
> and if so in what circumstances ... capital
> punishment, whether or not it violates s. 12 of the
> *Charter*, and whether or not it could be upheld
> under s. 1, engages the underlying values of the
> prohibition against cruel and unusual
> punishment... Its potential imposition in this case is
> thus a factor that weighs against extradition
> without assurances."[260]

These conclusions do little to give effect to and to ensure
the international or Canadian rights. Moreover, the Court
has introduced a worrisome devaluation of fundamental
Charter rights. At least for extradition:

> "The values underlying various sections of the
> *Charter*, including s.12 [protection from cruel
> treatment] form part of the balancing process
> engaged in under s. 7..."[261]

It is true that international rights are to be interpreted in
the context of the whole treaty. So in some sense, all rights
impinge on the adjudication of any one right. However, I
find it disturbing that the Court could reduce various
Charter rights into values and then to use them in a
balancing act of its own creation within *Charter s.7.* Surely
the intent of the *Charter* is to establish a set of autonomous
rights rather than to establish one right to be interpreted by
using a set of guiding values?

---

[260] *Ibid* para. 78.
[261] *Ibid* para. 57.

The international case law was clear by this time. The right to protection from cruel treatment is always at issue in adjudicating the death penalty. More than one right can be at issue. These rights remain distinct, each to be limited with care. It is true that an international treaty right is interpreted in the context of the entire treaty so that other rights are in some sense involved. But I can think of no examples in international case law where rights become "values" to be balanced within other rights. Provided the rights are from among the international rights that may be limited, any limit on each right must be established in law, for a legitimate purpose, necessary and proportionate.

The Supreme Court moved swiftly away from the life, liberty and security of the person part of the *Charter* s.7 right to consider what in the international human rights treaties would be the due process component.

> "... the respondents are deprived of their liberty and security of the person by the extradition order ... Their lives are potentially at risk. The issue is whether the threatened deprivation is in accordance with the principles of fundamental justice."[262]

The Court continued to interpret the *Charter* as before:

> "While we affirm that the "balancing process" set out in *Kindler* and *Ng* is the correct approach, the phrase "shocks the conscience" and equivalent expressions are not to be taken out of context or equated to opinion polls ..."[263]

---

[262] *Ibid* para. 59.
[263] *Ibid* para. 67.

In contrast with its early interpretation in *Singh*, the Supreme Court failed to give effect to international rights and international limits on the rights to life and liberty and security. The Court ignored its *Oaks* test, using instead its "balancing." It is reassuring that the Supreme Court added more objective factors to determine the conscience of Canadians:

> " ... The "shocks the conscience" language signals the possibility that even though the rights of the fugitive are to be considered in the context of other applicable principles of fundamental justice, which are normally of sufficient importance to uphold the extradition, a particular treatment or punishment may sufficiently violate our sense of fundamental justice as to tilt the balance against extradition. The rule is not that departures from fundamental justice are to be tolerated unless in a particular case it shocks the conscience. An extradition that violates the principles of fundamental justice will always shock the conscience."[264]

Part 7 of the judgment states: *"The Principles of Fundamental Justice Are to Be Found in "The Basic Tenets of Our Legal System."* Parts 8 and 9 of the judgement are lists of "factors" in favour and contrary to requiring assurances that the death penalty will not be applied before extradition. These factors include international rights and Canadian and foreign experience with the death penalty. However, there appears to be no principled rationale controlling the process. The meaning of "fundamental principles of justice" seems to float with the list of factors. At the end of the listing the Court simply states:

---

[264] *Ibid* Opening Summary of Judgment.

> "Reviewing the factors for and against unconditional extradition, we conclude that to order extradition of the respondents without obtaining assurances that the death penalty will not be imposed would violate the principles of fundamental justice."[265]

It is difficult to maintain a principled approach and a rule of law by balancing a multiplicity of factors and values in the middle of adjudicating a right. Also, one wonders what the point of *Charter s.1* is. It's role has vanished in this process. At the same time, in its reasoning on *Burns* the Court provided a large number of juridical and other factors against the death penalty, reminiscent of a similar long list provided in *Kindler* by dissenting Justice Cory with Justice Lamer who were arguing against expulsion to a real risk of torture. But the lists of factors appear almost incidental. The Court's reasoning did little to give effect to the rights at issue or to ensure the protection of these rights for everyone in Canada.

The weight of the "balancing" carried out by the majority of justices shifted from the position taken in the *Kindler* decision. This makes the judgment seem progressive. Only in exceptional circumstances would extradition be Constitutional without assurances from the receiving State that the death penalty would not be applied. However, in terms of international obligations, the evidence would have been better applied within the framework of a *Charter* s. 1 argument to show a shift in proportionality of the limit of a *Charter* s.7 and CCPR Art.6 right to life. Unfortunately, there were not interveners to press these points. The lawyers for Burns rightly chose the approach most likely to protect their client. At the time, the Council of Churches

---

[265] *Ibid* para. 124.

did not understand the relevance for refugees and non-citizen's rights of intervening to challenge the approach taken in the extradition of a murderer.

Burns may have had an impact on the UN Human Rights Committee. In any event, the UN Committee subsequently adjusted its own approach to the CCPR Art.6 right to life in *Judge* v. *Canada*. An issue, as the HRC saw it, was:

> "As Canada has abolished the death penalty, did it violate the author's right to life under article 6, his right not to be subjected to torture or to cruel, inhuman or degrading treatment or punishment under article 7, or his right to an effective remedy under article 2, paragraph 3, of the Covenant by deporting him to a State in which he was under sentence of death without ensuring that that sentence would not be carried out?"[266]

The HRC noted the arguments of the Court in *Burns* and went on to find that the extradition of *Judge* violated CCPR Art. 6.1 right to life and that the CCPR Art.7 right to protection from torture was engaged. Significantly, there was a second more difficult issue for the CCPR in HRC *Judge*:

> "The State party had conceded that the author was deported to the United States before he could exercise his right to appeal the rejection of his application for a stay of his deportation before the Québec Court of Appeal. As a consequence the author was not able to pursue any further remedies that might be available. By deporting the author to a State in which he was under sentence of death

---

[266] HRC, Judge, *Op.Cit. 2003*, para. 10.1.

before he could exercise all his rights to challenge that deportation, did the State party violate his rights under articles 6, 7 and 2, paragraph 3 of the Covenant?"[267]

The Committee found a violation of the CCPR Art.2(3) right to an effective remedy taken together with the CCPR Art. 6 right to life. There are individual committee member opinions on aspects of this judgment. Nonetheless, as with a court, the decision of the majority is especially significant. It indicates an HRC concern for the right to an effective court remedy to protect the individual from acts that may violate fundamental rights.

The main consequence of the Supreme Court's *Burns* decision in Canada was a shift in the normal outcome of Ministerial decision-making in the direction that an internationally argued judgment would have followed anyway. The Court did not ensure a remedy for any other individual's rights. The Minister remains free to choose his or her own exceptions. That is a problem. Governments seldom deprive members of majorities of key rights. They tend to target individuals in disadvantaged groups for rights violations. Ensuring rights can never allow the authorities to exercise discretion about exceptions. True, even fewer among the few people extradited to other countries with the death penalty may now have their rights violated. More people's rights will likely be respected and ensured as a consequence. Yet the HRC *Judge* decision shows rather clearly that, after *Burns*, the law does not meet Canada's obligation to ensure the right to an effective judicial remedy. It is no better for the exceptional, the hidden or the unpopular person who may be more in need of protection – like *Judge* or like *Ahani*.

---

[267] *Ibid* para. 10.7.

There is a disquieting political convenience in the approach taken in *Burns*. It supported Canada's abolished death penalty, it was obliquely critical of the US on the death penalty, it may have inspired improved international jurisprudence, but it avoided giving effect to rights to due process that might be costly and unpopular. It left administrative discretion free to exclude any selected "exceptional" individual. This possibility underscores the need for a Court that will ensure individual rights are protected from acts of authority. The Court moved no nearer to this in *Burns*.

Suresh in 2002

The Report about Canada in 2000 by the Inter-American Commission on Human Rights gave an authoritative international interpretation of Canada's obligations concerning deportation to risk of torture: it is never permitted. Canada had received similar advice in 1999 from the HRC about CCPR Art.7 protection from torture.[268] The case law of the UN Committee against Torture reinforced this same view about CAT Art.3.[269] As shown above, the

---

[268] "The Committee is concerned that Canada takes the position that compelling security interests may be invoked to justify the removal of aliens to countries where they may face a substantial risk of torture or cruel, inhuman or degrading treatment. The Committee refers to its General Comment on article 7 and recommends that Canada revise this policy in order to comply with the requirements of article 7 and to meet its obligation never to expel, extradite, deport or otherwise remove a person to a place where treatment or punishment that is contrary to article 7 is a substantial risk." Concluding observations of the Human Rights Committee: Canada. 07/04/99. UN Doc CCPR/C/79/Add.105, para 13.

[269] Brian Gorlick, "The Convention and the Committee against Torture: A Complementary Protection Regime for Refugees", 11 *IJRL* 479, 486-

HRC had decided that in extradition cases involving the death penalty, both the right to life and the right to protection from torture or cruel treatment or punishment were at issue. In *Suresh* the same rights arose in the very different context of deportation of a refugee. The central rights issue was a risk of torture. There was no way to avoid the *Charter* and international rights to protection from torture and the *Immigration Act*.

The court chose to focus on three issues: 1) did the Minister err in the exercise of her discretion? (2) Are the conditions for deportation in the *Immigration Act* constitutional? (3) Are the procedures for deportation set out in the *Immigration Act* constitutionally valid?

The facts are in the judgment.²⁷⁰ However the Ahani case had been joined to the *Suresh case* by the Court at the request of the government. The reasoning in *Suresh* was developed with the facts from *Ahani* also in the Court's mind. *Suresh* was a Convention refugee from Sri Lanka who applied for landed immigrant status. In 1995, the Canadian government detained him and commenced deportation proceedings on security grounds, based on the opinion of the Canadian Security Intelligence Service ("CSIS") that he was a member and fundraiser of the Liberation Tigers of Tamil Eelam ("LTTE"), an organization alleged to be engaged in terrorist activity in Sri Lanka, and whose members are also subject to torture in Sri Lanka. The Federal Court, Trial Division upheld as reasonable the *Immigration Act* s.40.1 security certificate with its legislated consequence of loss of liberty and deportation.

492, 1999.
²⁷⁰ *Suresh* v. *Canada*, [2002] 1 S.C.R, 2002 SCC 1.

Following a deportation hearing, an adjudicator held that Suresh should be deported. The Minister of Citizenship and Immigration, after notifying Suresh, the refugee, that she was considering issuing an opinion declaring him to be a danger to the security of Canada as provided in the then *Immigration Act* s.53(1)(b), issued an opinion on the basis of an Immigration Officer's memorandum and concluded that he should be deported.

Although the appellant had presented written submissions and documentary evidence to the Minister, he had not been provided with a copy of the Immigration Officer's memorandum, nor was he provided with an opportunity to respond to it orally or in writing. Suresh applied for judicial review, alleging that: (1) the Minister's decision was unreasonable; (2) the procedures under the *Act* were unfair; and (3) the *Act* infringed ss.7, 2(*b*) and 2(*d*) of the *Canadian Charter of Rights and Freedoms*. The application for judicial review was dismissed on all grounds. The Federal Court of Appeal upheld that decision.

The Supreme Court agreed to hear an appeal. The Council of Churches intervened alongside several other interveners. The Council of Churches argued:

> "the Federal Court of Appeal erred in holding that s.53 of the *Immigration Act* and the ad hoc process by which the Minister reaches a decision that a Convention refugee is a 'danger to the security of Canada' complies with procedural protections required under s.7 of the *Charter*. Refoulement to face a substantial risk of torture violates *Charter* s.7 and cannot be justified by s.1. The nature of the Minister's decision and its potential consequences ... require the highest level of procedural protection. Nothing short of a judicial model of decision

making will satisfy the principles of fundamental justice."[271]

The Council was hoping to build on the Supreme Court's use of *Charter* s.7 in the case of Burns. It was known that other interveners such as Amnesty International were focusing on the CAT Art.3, CCPR Art. 7 and corresponding *Charter* s.12 right to protection from torture. The Council focused on the due process. It expanded the arguments it had used in *Baker* concerning the elements for a fair process, again drawing on the dissenting decision of Justices Cory and Major in *Pushpanathan*. The dissenting decision read in part:

> "it would be unthinkable if there were not a fair hearing before an impartial arbiter to determine whether there are 'substantial grounds for believing' that the individual ... would face the risk of torture ... there must be an opportunity for a hearing ... and the hearing must comply with all the principles of natural justice. As well, the individual ... ought to be entitled to have the decision reviewed to ensure that it did indeed comply with those principles."[272]

The Council concluded its submission by asking the Court to allow the appeal and to strike down *Immigration Act* s.53(1)(b). Something comparable to this due process concern was subsequently taken up by the UN Committee against Torture in its examination of Canada.

The Supreme Court did allow the appeal. However, Suresh was only entitled to a new deportation hearing. The

---

[271] Canadian Council of Churches, Factum of the Intervener, Suresh v. Canada, SCC File No. 27790, para. 13, 14, 17.
[272] *Pushpanathan, Op.Cit. 1998,* para. 157.

Council's views were not adopted. The provisions of the Immigration Act were deemed constitutional. It was only the application of them by the Minister that was not constitutional. By its ruling the Court endorsed Ministerial discretion as the process to adjudicate one of the most fundamental international rights - protection from torture. The Court seemed less concerned about protection from torture than the possible risk to life. It said:

> "Deportation to torture may deprive a refugee of the right to liberty, security and perhaps life protected by s. 7 of the *Charter*. Section 7 applies to torture inflicted abroad if there is a sufficient causal connection with Canadian government acts. In determining whether this deprivation is in accordance with the principles of fundamental justice, Canada's interest in combating terrorism must be balanced against the refugee's interest in not being deported to torture."[273]

The Court found, on the role of courts:

> "We conclude that in reviewing ministerial decisions to deport under the Act, courts must accord deference to those decisions. If the Minister has considered the correct factors, the courts should not reweigh them. Provided the s. 53(1)(*b*) decision is not patently unreasonable -- unreasonable on its face, unsupported by evidence, or vitiated by failure to consider the proper factors or apply the appropriate procedures -- it should be upheld. At the same time, the courts have an important role to play in ensuring that the Minister has considered the relevant factors and

---

[273] *Suresh, Op.Cit. 2002,* Opening Summary of Judgment.

complied with the requirements of the Act and the Constitution."[274]

This position raises concerns about the international obligations. The Supreme Court position does not allow a court to adjudicate an individual's treaty rights or constitutional rights, and it does nothing to ensure that a court remedy will protect the individual from acts of the authorities which might violate fundamental rights such as a substantial probability of torture consequential to expulsion.

The Court concluded on constitutionality:

> "We conclude that generally to deport a refugee, where there are grounds to believe that this would subject the refugee to a substantial risk of torture, would unconstitutionally violate the *Charter*'s s.7 guarantee of life, liberty and security of the person. This said, we leave open the possibility that in an exceptional case such deportation might be justified either in the balancing approach under ss. 7 or 1 of the *Charter* ... We also reject the argument that s.53, by its reference to s.19, unconstitutionally violates the *Charter* guarantees of freedom of expression and association. Finally, we conclude that the procedures for deportation under the *Immigration Act*, when applied in accordance with the safeguards outlined in these reasons, are constitutional."[275]
>
> "... Applying these conclusions in the instant case, we find that Suresh made a *prima facie* showing that he might be tortured on return if expelled to Sri

---

[274] *Ibid* para. 42.
[275] *Ibid* para. 5.

Lanka. Accordingly, he should have been provided
with the procedural safeguards necessary to protect
his s.7 right not to be expelled to torture. He was
not provided the required safeguards. We therefore
remand the case to the Minister for reconsideration
in accordance with the procedures set out in these
reasons."[276]

The Court found on international obligations:

"Our concern is not with Canada's international
obligations qua obligations; rather, our concern is
with the principles of fundamental justice. We look
to international law as evidence of these principles
and not as controlling in itself."[277]

After such a position, it is difficult to see how the Canadian
government can argue before an international treaty body
that the Canadian courts ensure protection of the
individual's international treaty rights from the acts of the
authorities. The Court did not use international rights as
binding rights to be given effect and ensured by means of
Charter rights. Contrary to the Court's view, refugee
deportation to a real risk of torture is a different human
rights context from that of extradition to a death penalty
under a treaty. *Suresh* was not a convicted criminal being
extradited for a fair trial. *Suresh* was a refugee accused by a
secret process of presenting some secret risk to national
security. The Court had the opportunity here to revisit its
earlier notions about protection from cruel treatment in the
light of the authoritative international interpretation of
Canada's human rights obligations which had been
provided by the HRC in 1999. In the decision, the Court did

---

[276] *Ibid* para. 6.
[277] *Ibid* para. 60.

not to adopt the specific international advice about the absolute character of the prohibition of torture.

On the other hand, as if to distract from this ignoring of a fundamental international obligation, the Court provided an extensive review of international jurisprudence surrounding torture – correcting a number of lower court misunderstandings about the details of such jurisprudence. This correcting might be regarded as giving some effect to international rights. Yet in its principal findings the Court did not even speak of an international right in a treaty ratified by Canada to absolute protection from torture. Rather the court wrote of "an emerging international norm."

The failure of the Court to give effect to CAT Art.3, a binding treaty obligation, or to apply *Charter* s.12 is stunning when the right to protection from torture was so clearly central for *Suresh*. This is in sharp contrast with the right to life and the death penalty so central for *Burns*. The arguments developed for *Charter* s.7 right to life liberty and security of the person make far less sense for *Suresh*. For the Court, protection from return to a risk of torture was not given effect as a right. Rather the right became an emerging norm, as had happened to international rights previously when they became values in *Burns* and factors in *Baker*. The factor or value or emerging norm became part of the court's concept of "principles of fundamental justice" for which they are "evidence" for "balancing" while considering the right to life, liberty and security of the person.

The right to protection from torture is established as an absolute right – and indeed the Court took note of this in its reasoning. Canada accepted the absolute right to protection from torture as a treaty obligation and this Court is part of Canada. The central decision to be made and to be reviewed in *Suresh* was whether there was a serious probability of torture of Suresh as a consequence of the legislated procedure. I accept that the *Charter* s.7 right to life, liberty and security of the person is also at issue when protection from torture is at issue, via the rights to liberty and security of the person. However, the Court failed to make this link and so it could not correctly assess an appropriate limit on this right.

I find the balancing within *Charter* s.7 particularly inappropriate. It makes *Charter* s.1 redundant. It misses insights from the more principled *Charter* s.1 process for limiting the rights at issue – its *Oakes* test. That in turn misses exploring the legitimacy and necessity of deporting a particular refugee. It is worth recalling here my concern that a justification for limiting rights in *Charter* s.7 for a deportation differs from that for an extradition. The international test requires a legitimate purpose, necessity and proportionality. The balancing in *Charter* s.7 seems closest to determining "proportionality." However, other factors apply even in extradition. Indeed, the benchmark European Court of Human Rights *Soering* case hinged in part on the necessity of extradition to the U.S. There was an alternative possibility of extradition to Germany without risking the death penalty. By focusing only on balancing, the Court has taken it as given that to expel a refugee on grounds of national security is legitimate and necessary – which may not always be the case. Worse, the balancing seems unprincipled.

In addition to these general concerns, in *Suresh,* the person being deported is a refugee. The 1951 Convention applies to a refugee as the Federal Court of Appeal recognized. The evident purpose of the 1951 Convention relating to the status of refugees Art. 32 concerning expulsion is restrictive. It is to restrict expulsion to situations in which national security requires expulsion. Expulsion of a refugee may otherwise not be for a legitimate purpose. The Supreme Court decision was silent on this aspect of necessity. So that the 1951 Convention right was not given effect for other refugees. Hopefully, this was because the Court wished to focus on the key international rights at issue: CAT Art.3; and CCPR Art. 7 protection from torture. My point here is that even if one agrees that there may be cases in which refugee rights like life and liberty alone are at issue under *Charter s.7* and so might indeed be limited, the Court failed to thoroughly discuss *Charter s.1* and the legitimacy, necessity and proportionality of limiting these international rights, including the 1951 Convention right. The purpose of the security certificate procedure is to facilitate deportation. Yet it is not self evident that the imposition of the security certificate on a refugee with consequential limitation of rights must always be for a legitimate purpose and necessary.

The Supreme Court did little to ensure an effective remedy for international rights at issue. Under *Immigration Act* s.53.1, the minister could still deport a refugee to torture on grounds of national security. If there is a court process, it is the judicial review of this administrative decision. In the review, the Federal Court may only determine that the minister's opinion was reasonable and that the evidence presented was considered. The minister had to be patently unreasonable for a decision to be overturned. The American Declaration Art. XVIII right to resort to the courts to ensure respect for legal rights and to a simple, brief procedure whereby the courts will protect from acts of authority that violate any fundamental rights seems to have been ignored.

The Inter-American Commission on Human Rights gave some hint of its views in its 2002 admissibility report on IACHR *Suresh v. Canada*.[278] While the Supreme Court decision to send *Suresh* back for a re hearing dealt with part of Suresh's petition, it did not deal with the other rights allegedly violated by the security certificate and detention. As the Commission concluded:

> "The Commission, in this report, declares the petition admissible solely on the issues of Mr. Suresh's allegedly arbitrary detention, his access to a simple, brief procedure before the courts to ensure respect for his legal rights, and the alleged right to equality with Canadian citizens as regards the enjoyment of his liberty (Articles II (right to equality), XVIII (right to a fair trial) and XXV (right of protection from arbitrary arrest) of the American Declaration of the Rights and Duties of Man). The State takes the position that the detention was part of a deportation review process and that the delay was, in part, caused by the petitioner himself. The Canadian Courts have held the deportation review process and the concomitant detention to be constitutional and in lieu of a habeas corpus proceeding."[279]

I hope there is a timely decision on the merits of this OAS case, but fear a protracted process in which the Commission hopes the parties will reach a "friendly settlement." The Commission is probably hoping that the Supreme Court decisions from its June 2006 hearing of

---

[278] IACHR *Suresh v Canada*, Report N° 7/02, Admissibility, Petition 11.661, Manickavasagam Suresh, Canada, February 27, 2002, in Annual Report of the Inter-American Commission on Human Rights 2002, OAS Doc. OEA/Ser.L/V/II.117, Doc. 1 rev. 1, 7 March 2003.
[279] *Ibid* para. I2.

security certificate cases will pave the way.

In addition to the American Declaration right to life, liberty and security and to related due process, the UN Human Rights Committee found, in its own decision on *Ahani* v. *Canada* that in such a situation the special right of a non-citizen to present reasons against his expulsion, CCPR Art.13 was at issue. As noted earlier, the Committee against Torture, in its 2005 examination of Canada, specifically recommended that judicial review should be on the merits when expulsion to torture was probable.

The Court did pull back from some positions taken in the case of the former convict *Chiarelli* in the case of the refugee security risk *Suresh*. While it declared the *Immigration Act* to be constitutional, it implied otherwise. It said that more due process than the *Immigration Act* provided for was needed when a person showed a *Prima Facie* substantial risk of torture.

Ahani in 2002

Ahani was a citizen of Iran who came to Canada in 1991 and was granted Convention refugee status based on his political opinion and membership in a particular social group.[280] After arriving, the Canadian Security Intelligence Service (C.S.I.S.) began to suspect that Ahani was a member of the Iranian Ministry of Intelligence Security (M.O.I.S.), which sponsors a wide range of terrorist activities, including the assassination of political dissidents worldwide. The C.S.I.S. also believed that Ahani received specialized training in the M.O.I.S. that qualified him as an assassin. Shortly after his refugee hearing, Ahani was contacted by an intelligence officer from Iran, who is

---

[280] *Ahani* v. *Canada*, [2002] 1 S.C.R. 72.

alleged to be a commander of the M.O.I.S. Ahani arranged for a false passport, and met the commander in Zurich, Switzerland. From there, they traveled separately, but met again in Fermignano, Italy, which is apparently the home of a number of Iranian dissidents. Ahani returned to Switzerland, and then traveled to Istanbul, Turkey, where he obtained another false passport and returned to Canada. Upon his return to Canada, Ahani met with C.S.I.S. agents. C.S.I.S. alleges that during those meetings, Ahani admitted that his military training was part of his recruitment into the M.O.I.S., and that the intelligence officer he met in Europe was a previous associate. After receiving a report from C.S.I.S., June 1993, the Solicitor General of Canada and the Minister of Citizenship and Immigration filed security certificate with the Federal Court Trial Division, alleging that Ahani was a member of the inadmissible classes (ss. 19(1)(e)(iii), 19(1)(e)(iv)(C), 19)(1)(f)(ii), 19(1)(f)(iii)(B) and 19(1)(g) of the Act). Ahani was arrested (s. 40.1(2)(b) of the Act) and remained in jail nine years from June 1993 to deportation in June 2002.

Ahani challenged the constitutional validity of the security certificate process (s. 40.1 of the then Act) before the Federal Court Trial Division, which found the scheme to be valid in 1995, and an application for leave to appeal to the Supreme Court was dismissed. Ahani also challenged the reasonableness of the Security Certificate, but the court found that the certificate was reasonable, and that Ahani lacked credibility in 1998. Ahani was later informed of the Minister's intention to issue, in addition, a danger opinion (s. 53(1)(b) of the then Act). At the Minister's invitation, Ahani made submissions that he would be put at risk for having made a refugee claim and divulging information to the Canadian authorities with respect to his work with the Iranian government. Ahani denied the allegation that he was an assassin with the M.O.I.S.

Shortly after he made these submissions, an analyst with the Case Management Branch of the Department of Citizenship and Immigration, prepared a memorandum for both the Acting Deputy Minister and the Minister's consideration and attached Ahani's submissions together with other relevant documents. An opinion letter from the Minister's legal services unit accompanied that memorandum. The Minister then issued her opinion that Ahani constituted a danger to the security of Canada. Ahani filed an application for leave and for judicial review of the Minister's decision. Ahani raised a number of constitutional questions relating to the danger opinion (s. 53(1)(b) of the Act). Ahani also commenced an action in which he raised the same constitutional questions.

At the outset of the proceedings in June 1999, counsel for the Minister made a preliminary motion asking the court to apply the recent decision of Federal Court Trial Division in *Suresh* insofar as it decided the same constitutional issues and the motion was granted. On the remaining issues, the court concluded that there was ample evidence to support the Minister's discretionary decision that *Ahani* constituted a danger to the security of Canada. Note that the "ample evidence" on the matter of danger to the security of Canada that the Court refers to only has to show that the Minister's decision was reasonable, and that no technical error of law was committed that required court intervention.

Ahani appealed. In 2000, the Federal Court of Appeal dismissed all of the constitutional challenges. Ahani also sought judicial review of the Minister's opinion, but that application was also dismissed

The analytical framework of the Supreme Court focused on the distinct ministerial process for deciding to deport a refugee on grounds of national security as provided in the *Immigration Act* s.53.1. The court set a standard for court review of a Minister's decision to deport a refugee in *Suresh* repeated here saying:

> "... the standard of review is whether the decision is patently unreasonable in the sense that it was made arbitrarily or in bad faith, cannot be supported on the evidence, or did not take into account the appropriate factors. A reviewing court should not reweigh the factors or interfere merely because it would have come to a different conclusion...".[281]

Behind the scenes in both *Suresh* and *Ahani* was the security certificate procedure for non-citizens under the then *Immigration Act (1976)* s.40.1. Both *Suresh* and *Ahani* were a risk to national security because two federal ministers were of that opinion, and because the Federal Court determined that the opinion was reasonable given the evidence. However, in the security certificate process for a non-refugee, the person does not have access to all the information in the case against him or her, and the legislated consequence is mandatory imprisonment and deportation. It was because *Suresh* and *Ahani* were refugees that a minister had to make the additional s.53.1 decision - to deport despite the refugee status.

These two cases offered the Supreme Court the possibility to review the appropriateness of the *Immigration Act* s.40.1 procedures, which also include a Federal Court determination. The Supreme Court chose not to review and to nuance the lower court views on this matter that had affected the right to liberty of *Suresh* and *Ahani*. Thus the right to liberty, evidently limited by the detention resulting

---

[281] *Ibid* para. 16.

from the security certificate, and the rights to related due process and court protection were not given effect for the security certificate s.40.1 context.

The Inter-American Commission 2000 Report noted that Canada had advised the Commission that this s.40.1 certification process had been upheld by the *Chiarelli* case, had received favourable comment from the European Court of Human Rights in *Chahal* v. *UK* and that the Federal Court had quashed security certificates in some cases such as *Jaballah*. However, the Commission then went on to advise:

> "... the provisions of section 40.1 raise ... due process concerns under *inter alia* Articles XVII and XVIII of the American Declaration. First and foremost, where information considered within the process is withheld, the person concerned cannot be fully apprised of the case he or she is to meet. The legislation provides that the information at issue must be deemed relevant by the judge; however, its terms do not require an evaluation of the credibility or veracity of the original source, and the person concerned is unable to challenge the source to rebut the content of that information. Although the certificate review process is not criminal in nature, the non-disclosure of such information may well prejudice the rights of the person concerned, giving rise to serious consequences ... While the IACHR recognizes that the State is necessarily concerned ... to protect its ability to collect sensitive information, it is a fundamental principle of due process that the parties engaged in the judicial determination of rights and duties must enjoy equality of arms. A person named in a certificate who is the subject of secret evidence will not enjoy a full opportunity to

be heard with minimum guarantees, the essence of the right to due process. Both citizens and non-citizens must be accorded due process in the determination of basic rights, in this instance, the right to seek asylum and the right to personal liberty, in particular."[282]

In *Suresh* and *Ahani,* the Supreme Court made no comments about *Immigration Act (1976)* s. 40. It did not ensure an effective judicial remedy according to these international obligations. In fact, the Inter-American Commission 2000 Report is simply never mentioned in the judgment. The Supreme Court did rule that the standard to be met by *Suresh* or *Ahani* for a decision under the distinct s.53.1 is modified by the risk of torture consequential to deportation. So, only in the case of this refugee-related decision and its review:

"In circumstances where a Convention refugee makes out a *prima facie* case that there may be a substantial risk of torture upon deportation, the duty of fairness requires greater procedural protection than required by the Act under s.53(1)(*b*). In cases of that kind, a person facing a declaration under s.53(1)(*b*) and, accordingly, deportation to a country in which he or she may face torture, must be provided with all relevant information and advice produced for the Minister's consideration by the Department of Citizenship and Immigration and other sources, with an opportunity to address that evidence in writing and with written reasons. [283]

---

[282] Inter-American Commission 2000 Report, *Op.Cit.*, para. 157.
[283] *Ahani, Op.Cit. 2002,* para. 24.

Note "all relevant information and advice" is required to be disclosed. This requirement is consistent with the IACHR 2000 Report observations. Yet the due process for the decision to deport remains ministerial discretion. Access to court protection for the right is limited in s.53.1 by the threshold for review. The Court set out the consequences of this approach for *Ahani*:

> "When the analytical framework set out in *Suresh* is applied, the appellant has not cleared the evidentiary threshold required to access the protection guaranteed by s.7 of the *Canadian Charter of Rights and Freedoms*. The appellant has not made out a *prima facie* case that there was a substantial risk of torture upon deportation. ... In this case, unlike *Suresh*, the Minister provided adequate procedural protections. The appellant was fully informed of the Minister's case against him and given a full opportunity to respond. Insofar as the procedures followed may not have precisely complied with those suggested in *Suresh*, this did not prejudice him. The process accorded to the appellant was consistent with the principles of fundamental justice. Lastly, it was not patently unreasonable for the Minister to conclude that the appellant would constitute a danger to the security of Canada under s.53(1)(*b*) of the *Immigration Act* since there was ample support for the Minister's decision. There is also no basis to interfere with the Minister's decision that the appellant's deportation to Iran would only expose him to a "minimal risk" of harm. The Minister applied the proper principles and took into account the relevant factors."[284]

---

[284] *Ibid* Opening Summary of Judgment.

The Court acknowledged that Constitutional rights were at issue, yet did not ensure Constitutional rights. *Ahani* had a checkered history and unraveling the case posed a challenge. Yet human rights are intended to protect precisely this kind of person in this kind of situation. The Court implicitly accepted judicial review as an appropriate mechanism for respecting and ensuring and giving effect to rights and as the court process to protect a person's rights from acts of authority. Yet as presently practiced a court reviewing an administrative decision cannot call for additional evidence and cannot replace the decision with its own in order to ensure rights.

The Inter-American Commission 2000 Report is concerned about this aspect of review in the wider general refugee determination scheme:

> " ... because the [refugee] determination process cannot be reopened to present newly available information after the rejection of a claim, and because the scope of judicial review is limited to questions of jurisdiction and law, the judicial scrutiny of a rejected claimant's case on review may be incomplete if all the facts relevant to risk are not before the decision-maker."[285]

As noted previously, the Commission reminded Canada of a basic human rights obligation:

> "The American Declaration of the Rights and Duties of Man provides in Article XVIII that every person has the right to 'resort to the courts to ensure respect for [] legal rights,' and to have access to a 'simple, brief procedure whereby the courts' will

---

[285] Inter-American Commission 2000 Report *Op. Cit.* para. 106.

> protect him or her 'from acts of authority that ...
> violate any fundamental constitutional rights.'" [286]

The Supreme Court had an obligation to ensure protection for *Ahani*. That required examining the evidence and making the determination. In *Ahani's* case, submissions concerning a risk of torture were made, but there was never a hearing before an independent and impartial decision-maker about the risk of torture. The Supreme Court simply upheld the lower court review decisions on these matters. The "ample evidence" to which the Court refers merely showed that the Minister was not patently unreasonable in applying the security certificate. It did not mean the decision to deport was correct or even reasonable.

The Supreme Court ignored the obligation to "ensure" the international right to protection from torture for *Ahani* on the basis of no *prima facie* case. In contrast with the Supreme Court, reputable international bodies had little doubt that a *prima facie* case existed. They had publicly expressed concern about the risk of torture by the expulsion of Ahani. Amnesty International had asked the government of Canada not to deport. The UN HRC had written to ask Canada not to deport pending its examination of the case. The Court here preferred to follow the government's wishes than to ensure the fundamental rights of a less popular individual than *Suresh*. It is good politics to allow one case, *Suresh*, and deny another, *Ahani*, but it is not necessarily good law. It negates the whole reason for having a *Charter* of rights and international human rights treaties.

Within days of the Supreme Court decision, the request not to deport made by the UN Human Rights Committee was

---

[286] *Ibid* para. 95.

before the Ontario Courts.[287]

In both *Suresh* and *Ahani* the Supreme Court did not apply a formal human rights analysis. The Supreme Court failed to give effect to the international rights to protection from torture. The right to effective judicial protection from acts of authority that may violate rights was not given effect. To ensure the international rights, the Supreme Court would have had to require a different test for a reviewing court. It would have required all the elements of natural justice to be applied, as Justices Cory and Major argued in their dissenting opinion in *Pushpanathan*. The Council of Churches had put that position before the Court.

There is another international right at issue in these two cases. In its own subsequent decision *Ahani* v. *Canada*, the UN Human Rights Committee found that the expulsion of Ahani had violated Ahani's right to protection from torture taken with his right, as a non-citizen, to present reasons against his expulsion, CCPR article 13. This right had been implicitly granted to Suresh by the Supreme Court when it allowed Suresh to present his reasons. According to the HRC, there was no basis to treat Ahani any differently:

> "... where one of the highest values protected by the Covenant, namely the right to be free from torture, is at stake, the closest scrutiny should be applied to the fairness of the procedure applied to determine whether an individual is at a substantial risk of torture...this risk was highlighted in this case by the Committee's request for interim measures of protection." [288]

---

[287] *Mansour Ahani* v. *Her Majesty the Queen et al*, Ontario Court of Appeal, Judgment 17 January 2002, Docket: M28156/C37565.
[288] Human Rights Committee, *Ahani* v. *Canada*, *Op.Cit.*, para. 10.6.

> "... the failure of the State party to provide him ... with the procedural protections deemed necessary in the case of Suresh, on the basis that the present author had not made out a *prima facie* risk of harm fails to meet the requisite standard of fairness." "...such a denial of these protections on the basis claimed is circuitous in that the author may have been able to make out the necessary level of risk if in fact he had been allowed to submit reasons on the risk of torture faced by him in the event of removal, being able to base himself on the material of the case presented by the administrative authorities against him in order to contest a decision that included the reasons for the Minister's decision that he could be removed." "... as with the right to life, the right to be free from torture requires not only that the State party not only refrain from torture but take steps of due diligence to avoid a threat to an individual of torture from third parties." [289]

Recall, here, the longstanding importance of the equal treatment in the application of the non-citizen's CCPR Art. 13 right to present reasons against expulsion. Note too, that the HRC was critical of an aspect of the security certification process, finding a violation of CCPR Art. 9(4):

> "the Committee is prepared to accept that a "reasonableness" hearing in Federal Court promptly after the commencement of mandatory detention on the basis of a Minister's security certificate is, in principle, sufficient ... "... when judicial proceedings that include the determination of the lawfulness of detention

---

[289] *Ibid* para. 10.7.

become prolonged the issue arises whether the judicial decision is made "without delay" as required ... unless the State party sees to it that interim judicial authorization is sought separately for the detention. "... the "reasonableness" hearing lasted four years and ten months. "... part of that delay can be attributed to the author who chose to contest the constitutionality of the ... procedure instead of proceeding directly to the "reasonableness" hearing before the Federal Court, the latter procedure ... lasted nine and half months after the final resolution of the constitutional issue on 3 July 1997. This delay alone [9 ½ months] is ... too long in respect of the Covenant requirement of judicial determination of the lawfulness of detention without delay. Consequently, there has been a violation of the author's rights." [290]

On the due process standard for applying a Security Certificate, the HRC differed from the Inter-American Commission on Human Rights. The Commission, bolstered by jurisprudence of the American Court of Human Rights, required "equality of arms" so that the individual might see and counter the case against him or her. The HRC merely said, with respect to the CCPR rights:

" ... at the initial stage of the process ...the Federal Court's "reasonableness" hearing on the security certification the author was provided by the Court with a summary redacted for security concerns reasonably informing him of the claims made against him. "... In the circumstances of national security involved, the Committee is not persuaded

---

[290] *Ibid* para. 10.3

> that this process was unfair to the author. "... the Covenant does not, as of right, provide for a right of appeal beyond criminal cases to all determinations made by a court." [291]

However, the UN Committee against Torture, in its own Conclusions after examining Canada in 2000, had noted that the Security Certificate process was not adequate if used to deny access to protection procedures against expulsion to serious probability of torture. This was the *Ahani* situation.

In both *Suresh* and *Ahani*, the Supreme Court was challenged to ensure that the rights of the individual would not be violated by the acts of the authorities. It was challenged in a time of concern about terrorism. In Suresh, the court took a minimal step to protect him. In Ahani, it did not. It may be argued that after *Burns*, only in exceptional cases will persons be extradited to face a death penalty. Similarly, after *Suresh*, it is tempting to suppose that only in exceptional cases will refugees be deported to face a real risk of torture. The court judgments play to the layman's assumption that any remaining problems will affect a few individuals who are exceptions within a tiny group of non-citizens affected. Let us hope this is so. But it need not be so. Discretion remains the law for the minister - which means the authorities. They can choose whoever, whenever, becomes the exception.

The CCPR does not grant States the option to give some partial effect of their choosing to CCPR rights they select. The obligation is to give effect to and to ensure all CCPR rights for everyone. In this light, the outcomes of *Burns* and *Suresh* are not satisfactory. Also, it is not at all clear that

---

[291] *Ibid* para. 10.5

rights are ensured for the lesser extraditions and refugee deportations which do not reach public attention in high profile cases. In the lower profile HRC *Judge v. Canada* case, a violation of CCPR rights occurred in the context of a deportation to the death penalty. Without changes, further violations remain possible. Rights are not ensured.

The *Ahani* case leaves further disquieting questions. It revealed in a dramatic way the gap between the obligation to ensure international rights for everyone, including an individual plausibly accused of being an Iranian spy, and the approach of the Supreme Court. Subsequent activity in the Ontario courts about Ahani and about international rights in general deserves comment before this book reflects on what might be done.

Ahani at the Court of Appeals for Ontario

Ahani asked the Ontario courts to issue an injunction preventing his expulsion pending the views by the UN Human Rights Committee on his case. The majority at the Ontario Court of Appeal denied the request and gave little effect to the international human rights to protection from torture and to an effective court remedy. It followed the Supreme Court's lead on *Charter s.7*:

> "... even accepting a broad reading of the Supreme Court's finding, Ahani is still a Convention refugee... he still has a well-founded fear of persecution if returned to Iran. That is enough to trigger his s. 7 rights. In my view, however, even if Ahani's s. 7 rights are at stake, no principle of fundamental justice entitles him to remain in

Canada until his communication is considered by the Committee." [292]

" ... Ahani contends that the principles of fundamental justice include the right to remain in Canada until his international law remedies have been exhausted. ..." [293]

" ... He submits that once Canada grants an individual right, as it did by signing the Covenant and the Protocol, it must ensure a fair process and an effective remedy. Deporting Ahani to Iran while the Committee is considering his communication denies him procedural fairness and an effective remedy. ..." [294]

" ... The content of the principles of fundamental justice can only be determined by balancing individual and state interests. Here, Ahani's interest is reflected in the opportunity to seek the Committee's views on whether Canada's treatment of him breached the covenant. Canada's interest is reflected in two undisputed facts – two facts that show what Ahani seeks is not a principle of fundamental justice. The first fact is that Canada has never incorporated either the Covenant or the Protocol into Canadian law by implementing legislation. Absent implementing legislation, neither has any legal effect in Canada. Of course, Canada's international human rights commitments may still inform the content of the principles of fundamental justice under s. 7 of the *Charter*. But Ahani is not merely asking this court to interpret s. 7 in a way that is consistent with international

---

[292] *Ahani v. Canada,* Court of Appeals for Ontario, (2002), 58 O.R. (3d) 107, Para.27.
[293] *Ibid* Para. 28.
[294] *Ibid* Para. 29.

human rights norms. Instead, he seeks to use s. 7 to enforce Canada's international commitments in a domestic court. This he cannot do." [295]

The Human Right's committee has given its authoritative interpretation of a State's treaty obligations with respect to interim measures:

"By adhering to the Optional Protocol, a State party ... recognizes the competence of the HRC to receive and consider communications from individual claiming to be victims of violations of any of the rights set forth in the Covenant (Preamble and Article 1). Implicit ... is an undertaking to cooperate with the Committee in good faith so as to permit and enable it to consider such communications, and after examination to forward its views to the State party and to the individual (Article 5(1), (4)). It is incompatible with these obligations for a State party to take any action that would prevent or frustrate the Committee in its consideration and examination of the communication, and in the expression of its Views. ..."

" ... Interim measures pursuant to rule 86 of the Committee's rules adopted in conformity with article 39 of the Covenant are essential to the Committee's role under the Protocol. Flouting of the Rule, especially by irreversible measures such as the execution of the alleged victim or his/her deportation from the country, undermines the protection of Covenant rights through the Optional Protocol." [296]

---

[295] *Ibid* para. 31.
[296] Report of the Human Rights Committee, UN GAOR, 56th Session, Supplement No.40, UN Doc. A/56/40, Vol.1 (2001), paras. 128-30.

The views of the Committee have been noted and endorsed by Harrington who points to the *La Grande Case* of the International Court of Justice and its provisional measures order and to views of the Privy Council on interim measures as supporting jurisprudence.[297]

In the Ontario court *Ahani* case, there was some support for the international interpretation, but this support was only in the dissenting views of Justice Rosenberg:

> "... the removal of the appellant at this time to Iran, a place where he, according to the Immigration and Refugee Board, has a well-founded fear of persecution, is contrary to s. 7 of the *Canadian Charter of Rights and Freedoms* ..."[298]

> " ... by signing the Protocol the federal government has conferred jurisdiction upon the Committee. ... the non-binding principle goes only so far as to affirm that the Covenant and the Protocol do not create rights in the appellant that can be enforced in a domestic court. ... the appellant ... claims only the limited procedural right to reasonable access to the Committee ..."
> " ... the government having held out this right ... should not be entitled to render it practically illusory by returning him to Iran before he has had a reasonable opportunity to access it. ... it is a principle of fundamental justice that individuals in Canada have fair access to the process in the

---

297 Joanna Harrington, "Punting Terrorists, Assassins and Other Undesirables: Canada, the Human Rights Committee and Requests for Interim measures of Protection," (2003) 48 McGill L.J. 55, 72-81.
298 *Ibid* para. 76.

Protocol. By deporting the appellant to Iran, the government will deprive the appellant of this opportunity." [299]

" ... The basis for recognizing a due process right in these circumstances is based on more fundamental principles of due process. I find particularly attractive the dissenting speech of Lord Nicholls in *Briggs v. Baptiste*, [2000] 2 A.C. 40 (J.C.P.C.) at para. 47, where he said that he could not accept that "the law of Trinidad and Tobago is so foreshortened that the courts of Trinidad and Tobago must stand by, powerless to act, while Briggs is executed. By acceding to the Convention, Trinidad and Tobago intended to confer benefits on its citizens. The benefits were intended to be real, not illusory. The Inter-American system of human rights was not intended to be a hollow sham or, for those under sentence of death, a cruel charade." [300]

" ... In these reasons, I have accorded to the appellant a procedural right that the executive arm of government held out to him. ... But, the courts in their commendable effort to support the government's defense of this and other countries from terrorism must bear in mind the words of Justice Frankfurter in *McNabb v. U.S.*, 318 U.S. 332 (1942) at 347, which were adopted for this country by Lamer J. in *Reference Re Section 94(2) of the Motor Vehicle Act* at p. 310: "the history of liberty has largely been the history of observance of procedural safeguards." [301]

---

[299] *Ibid* para. 93.
[300] *Ibid* para. 98.
[301] *Ibid* para. 113.

Bouzari at the Court of Appeal for Ontario[302]

The case of Bouzari is a very different kind of case from those looked at so far in this essay. The case is important in that it reveals some of the thinking of an appeal court about the more general application of international law and human rights law to a case in Canada. It thus adds perspective to the reflection on the gap in expulsion situations and how that might be closed.

At issue in *Bouzani* was whether a person in Canada can litigate against Iran for a remedy for torture allegedly carried out in Iran at an earlier date. The Court of Appeal for Ontario accepted a role for customary international law and accepted that the prohibition of torture was a rule of *jus cogens*. The Court did this in a thoughtful and thorough manner. However, little was done by the judgment to advance particular human rights treaty rights and the effective judicial remedy for the individual.

> "... customary international law is generally defined as widespread and consistent state practice accepted as law. The immunity of states from civil proceedings in the courts of foreign jurisdictions is an example of a principle of customary international law. The enactment of the SIA [State Immunity Act] confirms that state immunity is a part of Canada's domestic law." [303]
> " ... A peremptory norm of customary international law or rule of jus cogens is a higher form of customary law. It is one accepted and recognized by the international community of states as a norm

---

[302] *Bouzari v. Iran,* Court of Appeal for Ontario, (2004), 243 D.L.R. (4th) 406.
[303] *Ibid* para. 85.

from which no derogation is permitted. Not only does the rule of jus cogens override other rules of customary international law in conflict with it, but, by the Vienna Convention on the Law of Treaties, a treaty obligation which conflicts with a rule of jus cogens is of no force or effect in international law." [304]

" ... The motion judge found that prohibition of torture is a rule of jus cogens. For the purpose of this appeal, no one, including the Attorney General of Canada, questions this conclusion. Rather the question is the scope of that norm. In particular, does it extend to a requirement to provide the right to a civil remedy for torture committed abroad by a foreign state?" [305]

" ... The motion judge conducted a careful review of the decisions of domestic and international tribunals and state immunity legislation and concluded that the peremptory norm prohibiting torture does not carry with it such an obligation. ..." [306]

" ... it is [CAT] Article 14 which is the focus of the appellant's argument. It reads as follows:
1. Each State Party shall ensure in its legal system that the victim of an act of torture obtains redress and has an enforceable right to fair and adequate compensation including the means for as full rehabilitation as possible. In the event of the death of the victim as a result of an act of torture, his dependants shall be entitled to compensation ... The question is whether this Article creates an obligation on a ratifying state to provide a civil

---

[304] *Ibid* para. 86.
[305] *Ibid* para. 87.
[306] *Ibid* para. 88.

right of redress for torture whether committed at home or abroad or only for torture committed within its own jurisdiction."[307]

The majority of the Court of Appeal panel noted that the motion judge had examined the provision in context of the treaty and then State practice and the majority concluded, with her, in favour of limitation of CAT article 14 to a State's own jurisdiction.

However, at the end of its 2005 examination of Canada, the relevant treaty committee, the Committee against Torture, gave Canada authoritative international advice on CAT article 14. At the end of its 2005 examination of Canada the Committee recommended:

> "...the State party should review its position under article 14 of the Convention [CAT] to ensure the provision of compensation through its civil jurisdiction to all victims of torture ..." [308]

If anything, one might conclude that the Canadian Courts will not interpret a possibly ambiguous part of a treaty without a direct clarifying statement or case law by the relevant UN Committee. But then, it is not clear whether the courts will even then go along with the interpretation provided by the treaty body. Certainly, there is little to lead one to expect any move from the positions established by the Supreme Court with respect to the application of the *Charter* to international rights of non-citizens in forms of detention or extradition or deportation as reviewed in this book.

---

[307] *Ibid* para. 72-73.
[308] Committee against Torture, "Conclusions and Recommendations ... Canada," UN Doc. CAT/C/CO/34/CAN, May 2005, para.5(f).

At this point, I provide my final summary of the views and recommendations from 2000 to 2005 about the binding human rights treaty obligations given to Canada by the treaty bodies. Note that all of the subsequent observations of the treaty committees have been given after the enacting of the *Immigration and Refugee Protection Act 2002.*

Summary of International Advice 01-05

The Committee on the Rights of the Child, examining Canada in 2003 expressed concern that Canada had not responded to some earlier concerns about asylum seeker and refugee children. These earlier 1995 concerns are set out at the end of chapter 4 and they focus on family separation by deportation as well as family unity in general. Some of these earlier concerns came before the Supreme Court of Canada in its 1999 *Baker* case.

The relevant 2003 concerns after the 1999 *Baker* case and the recommendations are:

> "... the Committee notes that some of the concerns previously expressed have not been adequately addressed, in particular, in cases of family reunification, deportation and deprivation of liberty ..." [309]

> "Refrain ... from detaining unaccompanied minors and clarify the legislative intent of such detention as a measure of "last resort", ensuring the right to

---

[309] Committee on the Rights of the Child, "Concluding Observations: Canada", CRC/C/15/Add.215, 27 October 2003, Para.46.

speedily challenge the legality of the detention in compliance with article 37 of the Convention." [310]
"Ensure that family reunification is dealt with in an expeditious manner." [311]

Canada's May 2005 examination by the Committee against Torture ended with a rephrasing of some concerns from the 2000 Concluding Observations and Recommendations, including concern about the failure to give effect to the international obligation to prevent torture consequential to expulsion, CAT article 3, and concern with inadequate preventative court procedures, that is, concern with what this essay calls the effective judicial remedy. Among the concerns is specific reference to "failure" and the case of *Suresh*:

> "the failure of the Supreme Court of Canada in *Suresh v Minister of Citizenship and Immigration* to recognise, at the level of domestic law, the absolute nature of the protection of article 3 of the Convention that is subject to no exceptions whatsoever." [312]

> "... the blanket exclusion by ... [*IRPA* 2002, s.97] ... of the status of refugee or person in need of protection, for persons falling within the security exceptions set out in the Convention on the Status of Refugees and its Protocols; as a result, such persons' substantive claims are not considered by the Refugee Protection Division or reviewed by the Refugee Appeal Division." [313]

---

[310] *Ibid* Para.47(c)
[311] *Ibid* Para.47(f)
[312] Committee against Torture, "Conclusions and Recommendations ... Canada," UN Doc. CAT/C/CO/34/CAN, May 2005, para. 4(a).
[313] *Ibid* para. 4(c).

"... the explicit exception of certain categories of persons posing security or criminal risks from the protection against refoulement provided by ... [*IRPA* 2002], s.115.2 ..." [314]

"... the ... willingness, in ... low number of prosecutions for terrorism and torture offences, to resort in the first instance to immigration processes to remove or expel individuals ... , thus implicating issues of article 3 of the Convention more readily, rather than subject him or her to the criminal process." [315]

In its recommendations, the Committee against Torture pointed out that when torture is at issue, a judicial review on the merits is called for:

"the State party should provide for judicial review of the merits, rather than simply of the reasonableness, of decisions to expel an individual where there are substantial grounds to believe the person faces a risk of torture." [316]

As noted in earlier chapters, the CAT case law has raised concerns about effective remedy indirectly while considering the admissibility of a case. These concerns relate to CCPR article 14.1 right to fair trial as well as American Declaration article XVIII right to fair trial and court remedy capable of adjudicating a fundamental right at issue. In *Enrique Falcon Rios v. Canada* the Committee

---

[314] *Ibid* para. 4(d).
[315] *Ibid* para. 4(e).
[316] *Ibid* para. 5(c).

against Torture observed:

> "... although the right to assistance on
> humanitarian grounds is a remedy under the law,
> such assistance is granted by a minister on ...
> humanitarian criteria, and not on a legal basis,
> and is thus ex gratia in nature." "... when judicial
> review is granted, the Federal Court returns the
> file to the body which took the original decision ...
> and does not itself conduct a review of the case or
> hand down any decision. The decision depends,
> rather, on the discretionary authority of a minister
> and thus of the executive. ... since an appeal on
> humanitarian grounds is not a remedy that must
> be exhausted to satisfy the requirement for
> exhaustion of domestic remedies, the question of
> an appeal against such a decision does not
> arise."[317]

> "... the principle of exhaustion of domestic
> remedies requires the petitioner to use remedies
> that are directly related to the risk of torture in the
> country to which he would be sent, not those that
> might allow him to remain where he is."[318]

> "... [As to] ... the State party's claim that the
> complainant could also have requested a review of
> the risks of return ... before being expelled ..." "...
> if ... an individual resubmitted an application for
> asylum that had already been evaluated by the
> Refugee Protection Division ... it would only be
> any fresh evidence that would be taken into
> consideration, and otherwise the application

---

[317] CAT, *Enrique Falcon Rios v. Canada 2004, Op.Cit.* para. 7.3.
[318] *Ibid* para. 7.4.

> would be rejected. ... this procedure would not
> afford the complainant an effective remedy ..."[319]

As already noted among the Supreme Court case law, the
UN Human Rights Committee gave its views on the
expulsion of Judge in part on account of the lack of access
to an appeal.

> "As to whether the State party violated the author's
> rights under articles 6 [life], and 2(3) [effective
> remedy] by deporting him to the United States
> where he is under sentence of death, before he
> could exercise his right to appeal the rejection of his
> application for a stay of deportation before the
> Québec Court of Appeal and, accordingly, could not
> pursue further available remedies ... the State party
> removed the author from its jurisdiction within
> hours after the decision of the Superior Court of
> Québec, in what appears to have been an attempt to
> prevent him from exercising his right of appeal to
> the Court of Appeal. It is unclear from the
> submissions ... to what extent the Court of Appeal
> could have examined the author's case, but the
> State party itself concedes that as the author's
> petition was dismissed by the Superior Court for
> procedural and substantive reasons ... the Court of
> Appeal could have reviewed the judgment on the
> merits."[320]

> "... in [HRC] *A. R. J. v. Australia*, a deportation
> case ... [the HRC] did not find a violation of article 6
> by the returning state as it was not foreseeable that
> he would be sentenced to death and "because the

---

[319] *Ibid* para. 7.5.
[320] HRC, *Judge v. Canada, Op.Cit. 2003,* para. 10.8.

judicial and immigration instances seized of the case heard extensive arguments" as to a possible violation of article 6. In the instant case ... by preventing the author from exercising an appeal available to him under domestic law, the State party failed to demonstrate that the author's contention that his deportation to a country where he faces execution would violate his right to life, was sufficiently considered. The State party makes available an appellate system designed to safeguard any petitioner's rights .... Bearing in mind that the State party has abolished capital punishment, the decision to deport the author to a state where he is under sentence of death without affording him the opportunity to avail himself of an available appeal, was taken arbitrarily and in violation of article 6, together with article 2(3) of the Covenant."[321]

The Human Rights Committee took the opportunity of its examination of Canada in October 2005 to review of number of concerns and to give advice:

"The Committee notes with concern that many of the recommendations it addressed to the State party in 1999 remain unimplemented. It also regrets that the Committee's previous concluding observations have not been distributed to members of Parliament and that no parliamentary committee has held hearings on issues arising from the Committee's observations, as anticipated by the delegation in 1999. (article 2)" [322] (para.6)

---

[321] *Ibid* para. 10.9.
[322] Concluding observations of the Human Rights Committee, Canada, UN Doc. CCPR/C/CAN/CO/5, 1 November 2005, para. 6.

In line with dissenting Justice Rosenberg in the Ontario Court of Appeal case of *Ahani*, the HRC noted:

> "The Committee notes with concern the State party's reluctance to consider that it is under an obligation to implement the Committee's requests for interim measures of protection. The Committee recalls that in acceding to the Optional Protocol, the State party recognized the Committee's competence to receive and examine complaints from individuals under the State party's jurisdiction. Disregard of the Committee's requests for interim measures is inconsistent with the State party's obligations under the Covenant and the Optional Protocol." [323]

On fundamental concerns about effective remedy and equal treatment the HRC continued:

> "The Committee regrets that its previously expressed concern relating to the inadequacy of remedies for violations of articles 2, 3 and 26 of the Covenant remains unaddressed. It is concerned that human rights commissions still have the power to refuse referral of a human rights complaint for adjudication and that legal aid for access to courts may not be available."[324]

Following the HRC *Ahani* case, the HRC now moved towards the Inter-American Commission on Human Rights about the security certificates under the *IRPA 2002*:

> "The Committee is concerned by the rules and practices governing the issuance of "security

---

[323] *Ibid* para. 7.
[324] *Ibid* para. 11.

certificates" under ... [*IRPA 2002*], enabling the arrest, detention and expulsion of immigrants and refugees on grounds of national security. The Committee is concerned that under such rules and practices, some people have been detained for several years without criminal charges, without being adequately informed about the reasons for their detention, and with limited judicial review. It is also concerned about the mandatory detention of foreign nationals who are not permanent residents. (articles 7, 9 and 14)."[325]

The HRC raised its concern about the absolute nature of the international right to protection from torture:

"The Committee is concerned by the State party's policy that, in exceptional circumstances, persons can be deported to a country where they would face the risk of torture or cruel, inhuman or degrading treatment, which amounts to a grave breach of article 7 of the Covenant."[326]

Unfortunately, this is not only a policy of the State party, Canada. It is the result of the current application by the Supreme Court of the *Charter*.

---

[325] *Ibid* para. 14.
[326] *Ibid* para. 15.

7. Taking the Measures Necessary

"the history of liberty has largely been the history of observance of procedural safeguards" [327]

By ratifying the CCPR, Canada promised "to adopt such legislative or other measures as may be necessary to give effect to the rights recognized in the present Covenant" and "to ensure to all individuals ... the rights recognized in the present Covenant" (CCPR Art. 2) Yet these rights cannot be enjoyed. They are at best values or factors influencing "fundamental principles of justice." The Court of Appeal for Ontario put it well in *Ahani*:

> "... Canada has never incorporated either the Covenant [CCPR] or the Protocol into Canadian law by implementing legislation. Absent implementing legislation, neither has any legal effect in Canada. Of course, Canada's international human rights commitments may still inform the content of the principles of fundamental justice under s. 7 of the *Charter*."

What measures need be taken? Confronted by a related lack of rights in law in the United Kingdom, the Blair government legislated the rights of the European Convention of Human Rights and Freedoms into British law.[328] For Canada, the equivalent convention would be the American Convention on Human Rights. Canada has also historically related to the UN human rights system.

---

[327] Justice Frankfurter in *McNabb v. U.S.*, 318 U.S. 332 (1942) at 347, adopted for Canada by Lamer J. in *Reference Re Section 94(2) of the Motor Vehicle Act* at p. 310, recalled by Ontario Court for Appeal judge Rosenberg in *Ahani* (in dissent), *Op. Cit. Ontario, 2002*, para. 113.
[328] Human Rights Act 1998, 1998 Chapter 42.

Fortunately, the American Convention came into force after the CCPR and is broadly compatible with it. Also, the regional Inter-American Court of Human Rights enjoys the authority to interpret other treaties such as the CCPR in this world region. Unfortunately, Canada has yet to ratify this Convention. Moreover, it is not clear that such a solution is strictly "necessary." As I will show, the *Charter*, as supreme law, could in principle ensure and give effect to several international rights.[329] Adjusting the existing *Charter* and tightening rules on its application may be all that is necessary.

As noted in chapter 1, the Standing Senate Committee on Human Rights became aware of a "gap" between Canadian and international rights law which this book has been exploring. It said little about obligations under the American Declaration. But it quoted the UN Human Rights Committee Report of 1999 in its own report:

> "The Committee [HRC] is concerned that gaps remain between the protection of rights under the Canadian Charter and other federal and provincial laws and the protection required under the Covenant [on Civil and Political Rights], and recommends measures to ensure full implementation of Covenant [CCPR] rights..."[330]

---

[329] "A country that has opted for an entrenched constitution has determined that there ought ot be limits on the kinds of laws that even a determined majority should be permitted to enact... They permit persons to challenge government decisions ... also because the law itself is invalid on grounds that it violates the provisions of the entrenched constitution. ... the constitution functions as a kind of "supreme law" against which ordinary legislation can and must be measured." Partick Monahan, *Constitutional Law, 2nd Ed.*, Irwin Law, 2002, 4.

[330] Standing Senate Committee Report, *Op.Cit.* 2001, 14.

The Standing Senate Committee was clear about the disjuncture itself and that one cannot expect the courts (and Supreme Court) to ensure full implementation of the CCPR rights alone:

> "The disjuncture between Canada's international human rights commitments and its domestic law cannot be allowed to go unaddressed. Nor is it either fair or proper to sit back and hope that the courts will rescue Canada from the inconsistencies of its approach to implementing international human rights. A new approach must be found."[331]

Obviously, measures to allow a greater awareness of international human rights and the authoritative interpretation of them would help. The HRC reminded Canada of that in its 2005 Concluding Observations noted at the end of the last chapter.

> "It [HRC] also regrets that the Committee's previous concluding observations have not been distributed to members of Parliament and that no parliamentary committee has held hearings on issues arising from the Committee's observations, as anticipated by the delegation in 1999. (Art. 2)"[332]

Publicity and public participation would help. The Standing Senate Committee itself could hold hearings. However, the Senate Committee recommendations do not affect the role of the courts or otherwise ensure international treaty rights. I summarize them as follows:

1. Appoint an ambassador as Canada's representative to the UN Commission on Human

---

[331] *Ibid* 14.
[332] HRC, Concluding Observations, *Op. Cit. 2005*, para. 6.

Rights.

2. Ensure Canada's outstanding reports to international human rights treaty bodies are submitted by 31 March 2002.

3. Have the Canadian Human Rights Commission conduct a human rights impact of security and counter-terrorism measures.

4. Amend the *Canadian Human Rights Act* to add "social condition" as a prohibited ground of discrimination.

5. Respond to the *Canadian Human Rights Act* Review Panel's 2000 Report ...

6. Consolidate international human rights instruments to which Canada is a party, as well as information on complaint mechanisms and make them accessible to Canadians via the Internet.

7. Hold consultations among federal provincial and territorial representatives to better implement human rights obligations.

8. Reinstate the practice of regular federal, provincial, and territorial meetings on human rights at the ministerial level at least triennially.

More focused direction is required if the Supreme Court is to ensure the individual rights promised in ratified treaties. At the same time, a State does not need to go beyond taking the measures necessary. Requiring that the *Charter* give effect to international treaty rights will be explored, but might not be enough. The record revealed in this book is that the *Charter* itself cannot always ensure international rights. Part of that related to differences in the detailed international rights promised with respect to the nearest corresponding *Charter* rights. Another part of the gap arose from lack of clarity about the priority a court sets on ensuring the rights of an individual. That too will be explored.

Van Ert, in his book, and Brunnee and Toope appear confident that the courts will adapt to applying international law in a principled way. But the evidence from the cases examined is not compelling. The Supreme Court now gathers principles and ratified and unratified treaty rights as values or factors to be bundled and balanced as ingredients of the principles of fundamental justice under *Charter s.7*. In chapter 1, I noted that Bayefsky had described in her 1992 book that the Court invoked international law to support a conclusion already reached by the court, but otherwise ignored it. The latest decisions could be described equally unkindly. Although somewhat optimistic about the role of the courts, the Senate Committee did not believe the courts should be left to solve the problem of the gap, and nor do I. The courts have not established a principled use of even CCPR rights over the more than twenty years since Canada's Ambassador Beesley told the HRC that *Charter* rights were similar to CCPR rights and would give effect to them. The courts remain almost totally silent concerning the American Declaration of Rights and Duties of Man, OAS customary law and the court remedies required in the OAS region of the world.

It is true that there is judicial training. But the academics views about the role of international human rights treaties are not coherent. A shift in public mood could push the courts. But I don't feel comfortable with courts which can be pushed by public mood. The government-dominated process for developing a degree of public consensus on an issue, described more unkindly as "manufacturing consent" by Herman and Chomsky,[333] should be distinct from a

---

[333] Edward S. Herman, Noam Chomsky, *Manufacturing Consent: The Political Economy of the Mass Media*, New York: Pantheon Books,

court ensuring the international rights of the individual.

In my view, taking the "measures necessary" to give effect to, to ensure and to ensure a remedy for rights in binding international human rights treaties calls for additional legislative action by Canada even if, as I hope, the courts will try harder anyway. This chapter first revisits some of the review of the *Charter* and international rights undertaken in chapter 2 with hindsight from the cases examined. It explores the extent to which the *Charter* might be a framework for ensuring international rights. The second part of this chapter then simply suggests the minimum changes to the *Charter* and the role played by the courts required to ensure international rights and a remedy for the individual.

Charter Potential: Rights and Issues

<u>Freedom of Movement</u>
(*Charter s.6;* CCPR Art.12)

The right to freedom of movement arose in almost all the extradition cases and in the *Chiarelli* deportation. Most cases were ultimately resolved on the basis of other rights at issue. In *Chiarelli* the Court implied that since *Charter s.6* allowed a distinction between citizens and non citizens with respect to this right, other rights did not apply for non-citizens with respect to their entering and remaining in Canada. The Council of Churches asked the Court to correct this *Chiarelli* impression in its intervention in *Baker*, but the Court had failed to do so at that time. However, the Court quietly moved beyond the position it took in *Chiarelli* in ruling on *Suresh*. It recognized that *Charter s.7* right to life liberty and security of person

---

2002.

applied. Further movement by the Court to fully correct *Chiarelli* seems possible.

The remaining gap is between the *Charter s.6* right to freedom of movement, which offers nothing to non-citizens, and the CCPR Art.12 right which extends to any non-citizen who can claim Canada is "his [or her] country". A long term resident and a stateless person should be able to enjoy this international right which remains open to further interpretation by the Human Rights Committee. In addition, refugee children and their families are owed related CRC Art. 9 and 10 rights to enter and leave for family reasons, as was raised by interveners in the *Baker* case. These, too, are not given effect by *Charter s.6*.

True, such international rights to freedom of movement can be "factors" in the discretionary humanitarian and compassionate process. The Supreme Court gave some effect to the CRC Art.3 best interests of the child principle in *Baker* in this way. However, CRC Art. 9 and 10 are by nature binding rights and the approach for dealing with a human rights "principle" used in *Baker* does not meet the obligation to give effect to and ensure these rights themselves. The Committee against Torture took a critical view in 2005 of the discretionary humanitarian and compassionate process relied upon in *Baker*. The H&C process was not an effective remedy for the right to protection from torture. That view seems to me to have some relevance for other uses where the humanitarian and compassionate process is used for the adjudication of important treaty rights. As the Senate Committee observed, the obligation to "ensure" a right is a strong obligation.

Wilson j. showed how *Charter s.7* might be used in her discussion of the right to security of the person in the case of Singh *et al.* This treats these rights as a little more like a right than giving them some effect as factors in the discretionary humanitarian and compassionate process. Yet use of a right as an aspect of liberty and security of person cannot ensure that international right itself. I see no alternative to adjusting *Charter s.6* so as to make it compatible with CCPR Art. 12.

Life, Liberty and Security of Person

(Charter s.7; CCPR Art.6 & 9; American Declaration Art.I)

As I have suggested throughout, to satisfy international treaty obligations *Charter s.7* must give effect to substantive rights to life, liberty and security of the person and to some due process rights. The American Declaration of Rights and Duties of Man Art. I has only a substantive right to life, liberty and security of the person. However, this substantive right links with the Declaration right to a fair trial for the adjudication of a right. CCPR articles 6 & 9 include substantive rights to life and to liberty and security of the person plus distinct subsections which specify forms of due process relating to the death penalty and to detention.

It is clear from the case of *Singh et al* that the Court could interpret *Charter* s.7 so as to give effect to all these aspects of the international rights in ratified treaties as I showed in chapter 2. However, from the earliest *Charter* extradition case of *Schmidt*, the Court chose to view *Charter s.7* as a balancing of a composite right to life liberty and security of person against fundamental principles of justice – a balancing in which the Court's view of what would shock the conscience causes the balance to tip. The swing from *Singh* was in part a shift from treating the "fundamental principles of justice" as containing at least the principles of natural justice - with access to due process and the courts and tribunals.

Following the shift in *Burns* towards objectivity in the "shock the conscience" test, it is conceivable that the Supreme Court might rediscover the natural justice component of the fundamental principles of justice as set out in the dissenting position of Justices Cory and Major in *Pushpanathan*, used by the Canadian Council of Churches in *Suresh*. However, to expect such a change without some measure is too optimistic. That will be taken up below.

As noted above, using *Charter s.7.* as a vehicle for other *Charter* rights and international rights like freedom of movement for non-citizens reduces rights to factors in "principles of fundamental justice." It robs the international rights of their nature as rights and of their distinctiveness. It reduces *Charter s.7* to a kind of grab bag, mixing important autonomous international rights and principles. The more factors added, the harder it is to be principled and to give a sense of rule of law. That seems to me to miss the point of giving effect to and ensuring international rights. Worse, stirring in other rights distracts from and weakens a focus of *Charter* s.7: the explicit civil rights to life, liberty and security of the person. That in turn weakens the ability to give full effect to and to ensure these fundamental international treaty rights.

Principles of Justice and Court Remedy
(*Charter s.7*, fundamental principles of justice
American Declaration Art. XVIII fair trial)

The American Declaration promises a right of access to a court to litigate a constitutional or American Declaration right. With hindsight, the Supreme Court showed in *Singh et al* how this American Declaration obligation might be made compatible with Canadian law: every non citizen involved in expulsion would be granted a right of access to a hearing by a quasi judicial tribunal backed up by a Federal Court review, with low threshold leave, on points of law. Clearly some measure is required to encourage the Supreme Court to interpret *Charter s.7* in extradition and deportation so as to meet international due process obligations.

The security certificate cases of Mohamed Harkat, Adil Charkaoui and Hassan Almrei, heard by the Supreme Court in June 2006, may bring *Charter s.7* case law closer to international obligations with respect to liberty. For these cases, the liberty will link to the *Charter s.10* right of *Habeas Corpus* taken up below. However, due process for other rights currently bundled into *Charter s.7* balancing is unlikely to be addressed by these cases. While theoretically possible, it is unlikely that the Supreme Court will shift to include natural justice within its principles of fundamental justice. That will require some other measure.

Liberty, Habeas Corpus and Detention
(*Charter s.10*; *Charter s.7*; CCPR Art.9.4; American Declaration Arts. XVIII & XXV.)

The main gap between *Charter s.7* and corresponding international human rights is a gap in the adequacy of detention review. As I suggested in chapter 2, the *Charter* meets the international obligations for *Charter s.7* liberty from detention if *Habeas Corpus* is the fundamental principle of justice which applies. *Habeas Corpus* applies as a right, not a factor. The Supreme Court decision in the case of *Reza* set access to *Habeas Corpus* for a non-citizen at the discretion of a lower Ontario Court judge. The decision left untouched the access by leave to the Federal Court for detention review. That leave had been deemed inadequate by the majority at the Court of Ontario for

Appeals in the case of *Reza*. However, this Ontario appeal view was avoided in the *Reza* appeal decision by the Supreme Court. There is an automatic stay of deportation pending *Habeas Corpus*. Such a stay must be requested under the Federal Court process. The process for leave used by the Federal Court was questioned by the Inter-American Commission on Human Rights in its 2000 Report. The Supreme Court left open the possibility of finding in a future case that the access to the Federal Court for review by leave was not equivalent to the access to *Habeas Corpus*. Making the Federal Court protection equivalent and of equal or lower threshold for access than *Habeas Corpus* would help ensure the international rights.

There is a related general issue. Equal access to *Habeas Corpus* is part of the general right to equal treatment before the law for non-citizens. It is taken up again below.

The June 2006 hearings of the cases of Harkat, Charkaoui and Almrei relate to the particular detention of those under a security certificate either as a non-citizen or as a refugee. The cases are somewhat similar to the HRC case *Ahani v. Canada* where the HRC found that the security certificate process violated Ahani's CCPR Art.9(4) right to court review of the lawfulness of detention within a reasonable time. Rather than dealing with such fundamentals, there is a greater possibility that the Supreme Court will endorse lower court decisions by allowing release of Harkat and Charkaoui with stringent monitoring conditions. However, these cases do not directly relate to non-citizen detention in general. So it is unlikely that the Court would give full effect to and ensure the relevant CCPR article 9(4) right and the American Declaration right. That would require changing the nature of the legislated Federal Court review process for any general detention of non-citizens. It would require a Supreme Court willing to strike down or modify the requirement for "leave" for review of non-citizen detention decisions and read in an automatic stay pending decisions. Alternatively, it would require a Supreme Court ruling that, to be constitutional, Federal Court detention review must be of equal threshold and equal content to *Habeas Corpus*. Such rulings are unlikely.

Protection from Torture

(*Charter* s.12; CCPR Art.7; CAT Art.3; American Declaration Art.I)

In its *Suresh* and *Ahani cases* the Supreme Court failed to give effect to the fundamental international rights to protection from torture when they were at issue. In its October 2005 examination of Canada, the HRC called on Canada to give effect to CCPR Art. 7. The *Charter* contains no express prohibition of torture, but it contains a prohibition of cruel treatment. In theory, the Supreme Court could have given effect to the international CCPR and CAT rights by viewing torture in its case law as an extreme form of cruel treatment which *Charter s.1* would never justify. Similarly, CAT Art.3 which prohibits expulsion to a serious probability of torture, could be given effect by application of *Charter s.12* protection from cruel treatment. However, the use of *Charter s.7* balancing seems entrenched at this point. Some measure is needed to give effect to and to ensure the international right to protection from torture per se.

Protection from torture itself has become such a fundamental international right over the last few decades that its absence from the *Charter* is an embarrassment. As a minimum, it should be added to the *Charter* together with the particular form of protection, CAT Art. 3, no expulsion to substantial risk of torture. Further measures to ensure such important rights are warranted.

Equal Treatment in Rights
(*Charter s.15*; CCPR Arts. 26 & 14.1;
American Declaration Art. II)

Non citizens have international rights to equal treatment before the courts. In HRC case law this applies at least for the adjudication of a fundamental right in substantially similar situations. In its *Ahani* v. *Canada* case, the UN Human Rights Committee found a violation of CCPR article 13 precisely because the Court did not grant Ahani equal treatment with Suresh.

In the *Andrews* case the Supreme Court failed to apply the international standard for equal treatment or non-discrimination. As noted in chapter 3, the Court of Appeal for Ontario, in the extradition case of *Philippines v. Pacificador,* ruled that the *Andrew* case precluded the right of equal treatment in substantially similar circumstances. As I noted in chapter 1, the end result for *Andrews* could have been reached by an interpretation of the *Charter* compatible with international standards.

In *Reza*, the Supreme Court left it to the discretion of a lower court judge whether a non-citizen had access to *Habeas Corpus*. Equal treatment before the law would require substantially identical treatment for a non-citizen and a citizen seeking the adjudication of *Habeas Corpus*.

Sharpe and Roach note the current test of the Supreme Court was established in the case of *Law v. Canada* which I introduced in chapter 3. They summarize it as : a) differential treatment under the law; b) on an enumerated or analogous ground; c) which constitutes discrimination.[334] These authors point out that the *Charter*

---

[334] Sharpe and Roach, *Op.Cit.* 2005, 276.

jurisprudence "is complex and it defies any attempt at a quick and accurate summary." Monohan agrees.[335] He notes that a simpler approach would have held that any law which imposes a burden based on an enumerated or analogous ground violates *Charter s.15*, requiring the government to justify the law under *Charter s.1*. He says Hogg also favours this simpler approach. That would give some effect to international non-discrimination rights. The Supreme Court did not explicitly rule out equal treatment in *Andrews* and it may be possible for the Court to add the equal treatment dimension, provided there is some measure to push in this direction.

Here, I must comment on the historic preoccupation of successive Canadian governments with the cost of giving non-citizens the justice promised by international treaty rights. At first glance, the cost of a general equal treatment ruling might be presumed to be prohibitive. However, on reflection, the cost of imposing an equal treatment obligation is more likely marginal. It would be just another factor for officials and tribunal members who are already responsible for carrying out administrative law. It would be just another factor for courts already reviewing decisions. It might take a little longer to make the decisions, but it would not require any major restructuring of administrative law. Certainly, allowing the few individuals falling under a security certificate to access the tribunal hearing (Immigration Appeal Division) available to other non-citizens is a minor marginal cost. The Court has already imposed requirements on administrative decision making in *Baker* and on judicial review in both *Pushpanathan* and in *Baker*. This imposition would be different in degree, but not so different in kind. The equal treatment in access to courts, taken up below, would be

---

[335] Monahan, *Op.Cit* 2002, 436.

limited to situations when comparable rights are at issue. How to ensure the Supreme Court takes such a step is the real question.

Family Rights and Children's Rights
(*Charter* s.7; CCPR Art. 17, 23 & 24; CRC Art. 3, 9 & 10; American Declaration Art. V, VI & VII)

In *Baker* the Supreme Court reduced children's rights to "factors" to be taken into account in discretionary administrative decision-making. The impact is on non-citizens in deportation or entry situations who have well developed family ties to Canada. The HRC view became clearer and more consistent in the mid 1990s before the *Baker* case, and the Inter-American Commission view became clear in 2000, just after the case. International family rights and children's rights can be violated by deportation. The Inter-American Commission on Human Rights advised that it will be only in exceptional circumstances that it will be proportionate for an OAS member State to limit these rights by deportation of long term residents.

The Supreme Court's decision in *Baker* did allow the administrative authorities to apply the evolving clarified international case law as an evolving factor. However, ensuring the international rights is an obligation and their present use as factors in discretionary decision making is inadequate. It does not satisfy the due process obligations for adjudicating a family or children's right from the American Declaration of Rights and Duties of Man. The Federal Court review does not serve as an effective court remedy capable of ensuring these rights, equally.

The Council of Churches intervention in the *Baker* case suggested the *Charter* s.7 right to life, liberty and security of person could be interpreted so that families and children of non-citizens in extradition or deportation enjoy the same "liberty interest" that the Supreme Court has determined that children of citizens in Canada enjoy when the State proposes their separation from their families for foster care. Treating an international right as an aspect of "liberty" is distinct from adding it to the bundles of factors within "principles of fundamental justice" to be balanced, but it is still not good enough.

I have argued above that using one right as a vehicle for giving effect to another simply cannot give full effect to either right. The international rights are distinct. Giving them equal effect with other rights and ensuring them and providing a remedy for them equally as rights requires some clear articulation of these rights in the *Charter*. The CCPR, CRC and American Declaration family and children's rights are quite similar and quite compatible, so that drafting one or two additional *Charter* rights to give effect to these distinct rights would not appear too problematic.

Effective (Court) Remedy
(*Charter s. 7 & 10*; CCPR Arts.2.3, 9.4 & 14.1;
American Declaration Arts. XVIII & XXV)

A due process gap has arisen in international cases in extradition, in deportation, in detention review under the security certificate regime, in refugee status determination and in pre-removal risk review. Presently, the *Immigration and Refugee Protection Act 2002* requires non citizens to seek leave, that is ask permission of the court. The Supreme Court has consistently ruled that the federal laws governing deportation and extradition comply with the *Charter*. The Minister or officials decide on deportation to torture or on extradition to the death penalty. Officials decide when family rights and children's rights are at issue.

American Declaration Art. XVIII requires a fair trial for the adjudication of rights and a simple effective court remedy to protect the individual from acts of the authorities which may violate rights – conditions which a Minister or an official cannot satisfy. The Inter-American Commission has expressed concerns about the threshold of the "leave" requirement. CCPR Art. 2 requires that all rights be ensured and an effective remedy provided.

To meet the international obligations, a court must be able to ensure the fundamental rights of the individual before it. A decision on the merits from a court is required at some level. This was a concern of the UN Committee against Torture in its examination of Canada in 2000 and again in the CAT *Enrique Falcon Rios* v. *Canada*. The Committee against Torture found that judicial review with a standard of "correctness" on the merits was required to satisfy the obligation to ensure an absolute protection from torture when torture is a substantial probability following an administrative decision to expel. In the *Falcon Rios* case, the CaT also found that the application to remain on humanitarian and compassionate grounds was not an effective remedy for protection against expulsion to a serious probability of torture. The administrative procedures which aim to protect from deportation to torture were inadequate because the procedure cannot examine all of the evidence involved – only new evidence arising since the refugee status hearing. This same issue was a concern of the Inter-American Commission on Human Rights in its 2000 Report on Canada.

The HRC *Ahani* v. *Canada* case shows that CCPR Art. 13 right of the non-citizen to give reasons against expulsion includes some aspects of fair trial and, in particular, that equal treatment is important. In the HRC *Judge v. Canada* deportation case, the HRC implied a similar equal treatment in access to a court appeal procedure. If a court remedy exists and fundamental rights are involved, the person must be given the opportunity to try that court remedy. These international concerns can be met by easy access to a court review with a standard of correctness on the merits.

Allowing every non citizen in expulsion access to the combination of existing quasi judicial tribunal (IAD) plus court judicial review along the lines of the *Singh et al* decision might be adapted to meet the international rights due process obligations. That is far from current case law, but quite feasible. As noted in chapter 4, prior to *Chiarelli* and subsequent legislative changes of the 1990s, non citizens could raise *Charter* rights and other rights at issue in their expulsion before what was then the Immigration Appeal Board. General access for all non-citizens to such a hearing gives clear and unambiguous effect to the CCPR article 13 right of the non-citizen to present reasons against expulsion. Combined with a lower threshold for leave to appeal, it would give effect to the American Declaration right to a fair trial for the adjudication of a right and to access a court for the protection of rights.

Charter s.24(1) presently lacks the force of the American Declaration right, repeated above, and of the CCPR Art. 2 obligation to ensure rights and ensure an effective remedy for them. The *Charter* simply says:

> "Anyone whose rights ... have been infringed or denied may apply to a court of competent jurisdiction to obtain such remedy as the court considers appropriate and just in the circumstances ..."

Also, as noted earlier, the jurisprudence surrounding *Charter s.24(1)* may itself be an obstacle.[336] Adjusting this language to give greater direction to the court to ensure the protection of rights is surely one of the "measures, legislative if necessary."

<u>Applying the Charter</u>

A feature in the Court's recent history on the matter of due process rights has been the Court's failure to consider *Charter* rights before it.[337] When *Charter* rights are not engaged, these *Charter* rights cannot be used to give effect to international human rights. The Court also defined the standard for standing of interveners, that is, their permission to be heard before a court, in *Canadian Council of Churches v. M.E.I.* in 1992 such that it did not hear concerns about provisions of the *Immigration Act,* as amended in 1989 that violated international rights.

In theory, this standing issue and the obligation of the Court to apply the *Charter* so as to ensure international rights could be modified by the Court itself. In the more recent *Vriend* case the Supreme Court reached a different conclusion about standing for interveners. However, the Court's decision about standing to allow equal rights for gays does not imply its application to allow rights of non citizens in expulsion.

---

[336] See Hogg's comment in chapter 2 that the wording of *Charter s.24* has been interpreted to require a high threshold for standing from an individual seeking a remedy for the violation of a right.

[337] See Beatty's observation reported in Chapter 1. See Supreme Court on *Chiarelli, Baker, Suresh, Ahani.*

In summary, the obligation to ensure the international rights for non-citizens in detention, extradition and deportation requires further measures to ensure courts will apply international rights through the *Charter*, as well as further measures to add missing international rights to the *Charter*.

Ways Forward

International rights by reference

There has been one measure taken towards giving the courts direction with respect to international rights in an immigration context. The federal parliament incorporated international human rights treaty obligations by reference into the *Immigration and Refugee Protection Act 2002* in s.3(3)(f). This seems timid when all provincial governments and the federal government agreed to almost every international human rights treaty obligation. Unfortunately, the reference in the *IRPA 2002* does little to help other potential victims of Canadian law in other areas, such as extradition. Also, the same *IRPA 2002* which allows for the possibility of implementing international rights also sets out measures, for example the security certificate process, which are substantially similar to those in the *Immigration Act* and which were found to inadequately protect international rights as determined by the treaty bodies.

The *Charter* is the most relevant Canadian law about rights and the only vehicle to give effect to and to ensure a CCPR or American Declaration right as a right binding on Canada. The Supreme Court has shown by *Singh et al* and by *Chiarelli* that it can find ways to either follow international rights or to ignore them, so long as its present flexibility of action remains. To ensure international rights requires more than a reference in one or two laws whose other detailed provisions challenge international human rights obligations. Making explicit in the *Charter* itself that the *Charter* is intended to give effect to Canada's international human rights treaty obligations is necessary to close much of the gap with international jurisprudence. It would restore the original expectations of the *Charter*. It would allow the Court to begin to change patterns arising in its past case law.

I made the case that the Charter should include the relevant international rights as rights. In parallel with adding such a reference, the *Charter* text itself should be adjusted. It should refer to protection from torture as well as cruel treatment. *Charter s.6* freedom of movement should match the CCPR Art. 12 right. Family and children's rights should be added, compatible with both the American Declaration rights and CCPR Art. 17, 23, 24. There will also be a need to adjust *Charter s.24* to mandate the courts to ensure and to protect *Charter* rights when individual apply to them. Of course, more changes to the *Charter* would be desirable, but the obligation on Canada requires only taking the measures necessary. Obtaining the support of the Canadian provinces for such a reference to international human rights obligations in the *Charter* should be possible. The provinces agreed to almost all the international treaties ratified by the federal government.

<u>A court mandate to protect rights</u>

The second part of the answer to the question of what is necessary to ensure the international rights as rights is to clarify the expected role of the courts.

As noted above, *Charter s.24(1)* should be adjusted to require a protection role from a court with respect to an individual's *Charter* rights – and *Charter* rights would, by reference, give protection for corresponding international treaty human rights. To my mind this appears a "necessary" measure and it may be feasible.

However, the role of the Supreme Court itself is crucial and as I showed in chapter 2 the mandate of the Supreme Court is set out in the *Supreme Court Act*. The CCPR requires Canada to ensure the CCPR rights. The American Declaration requires court protection for rights. The Supreme Court should be required to ensure *Charter* rights of an individual before it and to ensure lower court processes are such as to protect the individual from a potential violation of *Charter* rights, even by acts of the authorities. The *Charter* rights would incorporate international treaty human rights by reference.

The Supreme Court is a federal court with several important functions which may or may not involve applying the *Charter*. Changing the nature of the Supreme Court into a human rights court does not appear as essential as giving the Court clear direction to apply the *Charter* so as to give effect to the binding international rights. A better judicial appointment process is required so as to ensure the right to fair trial by an independent and impartial judiciary. However, this in itself is not sufficient to deal with the role the Supreme Court must play in ensuring individual rights if future case law is to become consonant with international treaty obligations.

Of course, there are cost implications. Few would challenge constant efforts to seek greater efficiency. At the same time, taking the measures necessary obviously brings costs. Canada implicitly agreed to pay when it ratified the human rights treaties. This need not mean that costs would have to be more than a marginal increase. The Supreme Court could have its priorities reset, and then be funded to deliver that marginal extra work.

Having a Constitution which places a premium on the rights of the individual in need is timely. Alongside greater measures to apprehend individuals suspected of links to terrorism, there should be greater means for the promotion and protection of individual rights - distanced from the political interests of any one government of the moment in Canada and from the political pressures of the powerful neighbour to the South.

While it is not strictly necessary to change the nature of the Supreme Court, I find it incongruous that a Supreme Court overseeing a Constitution is governed by a *Supreme Court Act* that is the product of only one of the parties involved - the federal parliament. In the longer term, one might suppose that the content of the *Supreme Court Act*, modified in negotiation with the provinces, might be incorporated into the *Constitution Act*. The Supreme Court would then formally belong to all partners comprising Canada.

Additional Measures

In addition, there have been other suggestions that might help to ensure treaty rights. I noted some at the beginning of this chapter. In addition, in its 2000 Report, the Inter-American Commission on Human Rights noted the various ways that the OAS system might help Canada. Similarly, the Office of the UN High Commissioner for Human Rights and the Office for Democratic Institutions and Human Rights of the Organization for Cooperation and Security in Europe can all provide advisory services for legislation.

Beyond such measures, the Standing Senate Committee on Human Rights issued two reports suggesting that Canada should ratify the American Convention on Human Rights.[338] This seemingly separate initiative might offer a moment of opportunity for the other changes suggested above. Clearly this is not the answer in itself. Other treaties have brought obligations that have been ignored. However, the American Convention brings exciting possibilities. In the longer term, decisions from the Inter-American Court of Human Rights could add reasoned international perspectives to Canadian law with the sense of authority which comes from a court. That would provide the Supreme Court with valuable international support for the proposed clarified role in this book - giving effect to and ensuring international rights for individuals before it. Canada is a middle power next to a super power. Drawing on the authority of an arms length regional body for the protection of the rights of the individual in Canada could be a wise move – if not a necessary measure to give effect to and to ensure international human rights obligations.

In the end, ensuring rights for non-citizens can only strengthen the safeguards promised for Canadians in their own hours of need in the age of the war against terrorists.

---

[338] In May 2005, the Senate Committee issued an interim report reviewing its 2003 report "Enhancing Canada's Role in the OAS: Canadian Adherence to the American Convention on Human Rights" recommending again that Canada ratify the American Convention on Human Rights by July 28, 2008.

Bibliography

David Beatty, *Constitutional Law in Theory and Practice*, Toronto, Buffalo, London: University of Toronto Press, 1995.

Anne F. Bayefsky, *International Human Rights Law: Use in Canadian Charter of Rights and Freedoms Litigation*, Butterworths, Toronto/Vancouver, 1992.

Mark Freeman & Gibran Van Ert, *International Human Rights Law*, Toronto: Irwin Law, 2004.

Mark Freeman & Giran Van Ert, *International Human Rights Law: Texts, Cases, and Materials*, Toronto: Irwin Law, 2005.

James C. Hathaway, *The Rights of Refugees under International Law*, Cambridge: Cambridge University Press, 2005.

Edward S. Herman, Noam Chomsky, *Manufacturing Consent: The Political Economy of the Mass Media*, New York: Pantheon Books, 2002.

Peter W. Hogg, *Constitutional Law of Canada*, Student Edition 2003, Toronto:Thomson Canada, 2003.

Inter-American Commission on Human Rights, "Report on the Situation of Human Rights of Asylum Seekers within the Canadian Refugee Determination System, OAS doc. OEA/Ser.L/V/II.106, Doc.40 rev., Feb. 28, 2000.

Ninette Kelley and Michael Trebilcock, *The Making of the Mosaic: A History of Canadian Immigration Policy*, Toronto/Buffalo/London: University of Toronto Press, 1998.

David Matas with Ilana Simon, *Closing the Doors: The Failure of Refugee Protection "*, Toronto: Summerhill Press, 1989.

Peter McCormick, *Supreme at Last: The Evolution of the Supreme Court of Canada*, Toronto: James Lorimer & Company Ltd., 2000.

Patrick Monohan, *Constitutional Law*, 2nd Ed., Toronto, Irwin Law, 2002.

Manfred Nowak, *UN Covenant on Civil and Political Rights: CCPR Commentary*, N. P. Engel: Kehl/Strasbourg/Arlington, 1993.

Robert J. Sharpe, Kent Roach, *The Charter of Rights and Freedoms*, 3rd Ed., Toronto: Irwin Law, 2005.

Gibran Van Ert, *Using International Law in Canadian Courts*, The Hague: Kluwer Law International, 2002.

David Weissbrodt, *Final Report on the Rights of Non-Citizens*, U.N. Doc. E/CN.4/Sub.2/2003/23 (2003).

Index

Index

Index

Index

www.ingramcontent.com/pod-product-compliance
Lightning Source LLC
Chambersburg PA
CBHW061346280526
45784CB00001B/147